MW00779503

BHAGAVAD GITA in a Nutshell

J. P. Vaswani

Published by:
GITA PUBLISHING HOUSE
Sadhu Vaswani Mission,
10, Sadhu Vaswani Path,
Pune - 411 001, (India).
gph@sadhuvaswani.org

FOR PRIVATE CIRCULATION ONLY

BHAGAVAD GITA IN A NUTSHELL
©2013, J. P. Vaswani
ISBN: 978-93-80743-75-2
1st Edition – 4000 copies – September, 2011
2nd Edition– 4000 copies – January, 2014

DADA VASWANI'S BOOKS
Visit us online to purchase books on self-improvement, spiritual
advancement, meditation and philosophy.
Plus audio cassettes, CDs, DVDs, monthly journals and books in Hindi.
www.dadavaswanisbooks.org

Printed by:
MEHTA OFFSET PVT. LTD.
Mehta House,
A-16, Naraina Industrial Area II,
New Delhi - 110 028. (India).
info@mehtaoffset.com

BHAGAVAD GITA in a Nutshell

J. P. Vaswani

Gita Publishing House
PUNE, (India).
www.dadavaswanisbooks.org

Books and Booklets by J.P. Vaswani

7 Commandments of the Bhagavad Gita

10 Commandments of a Successful Marriage

100 Stories You Will Never Forget

108 Pearls of Practical Wisdom

108 Simple Prayers of a Simple Man

108 Thoughts on Success

114 Thoughts on Love

A Little Book of Life

A Little Book of Wisdom

A Simple and Easy Way To God

A Treasure of Quotes

Around The Camp Fire

Be An Achiever

Be in the Driver's Seat

Begin the Day with God

Burn Anger Before Anger Burns You

Comrades of God - Lives of Saints from East & West

Daily Appointment with God

Daily Inspiration (A Thought for Every Day of The Year)

Daily Inspiration

Destination Happiness

Dewdrops of Love

Does God Have Favorites?

Finding Peace of Mind

Formula for Prosperity

Friends Forever

Gateways to Heaven

God In Quest of Man

Good Parenting

How to Overcome Depression

I am a Sindhi

I Luv U, God!

India Awake

Joy Peace Pills

Kill Fear Before Fear Kills You

Ladder of Abhyasa

Lessons Life Has Taught Me

Life after Death

Life and Teachings of Sadhu Vaswani

Life and Teachings of the Sikh Gurus: Ten Companions of God

Living in the Now

Management Moment by Moment

Mantras for Peace of Mind

Mantra for the Modern Man

Many Paths: One Goal

Many Scriptures: One Wisdom

Nearer, My God, To Thee!

New Education Can Make the World New

Peace or Perish: There Is No Other Choice

Positive Power of Thanksgiving

Questions Answered

Saints For You and Me

Saints With A Difference

Say No to Negatives

Secrets of Health And Happiness

Shake Hands With Life

Short Sketches of Saints Known & Unknown

Sketches of Saints Known & Unknown

Spirituality in Daily Life

Stop Complaining: Start Thanking!

Swallow Irritation Before Irritation Swallows You

Teachers are Sculptors

The Goal Of Life and How To Attain It

The Highway To Happiness

The Little Book of Freedom from Stress

The Little Book of Prayer

The Little Book of Service

The Little Book of Success

The Little Book of Yoga

The Magic of Forgiveness

The Miracle of Forgiving

The New Age Diet: Vegetarianism for You and Me

The Perfect Relationship: Guru and Disciple

The Terror Within

The Way of Abhyasa

Thus Have I Been Taught

Tips For Teenagers

What You Would Like To know About Karma

What You Would Like To know About Hinduism

What to Do When Difficulties Strike: 8 easy Practical Suggestions.

Why Do Good People Suffer?

Women: Where Would the World Be Without You

You Are Not Alone: God Is With You!

You Can Change Your Life: Live— Don't Just Exist!

Why Be Sad?

Contents

Foreword

Whenever I reflect on the Gita, my heart feels a thrill of devotion for Sri Krishna, the Divine Lord who came to live amongst mortals with His Message; and I bow my head in lowly reverence to my beloved Gurudev, Sadhu Vaswani, whom I regard as the 'Supreme Yogi' so beautifully described in the Gita.

Gurudev Sadhu Vaswani spoke to us on the Gita: he translated the Gita into Sindhi and English. He wrote much on the Gita. Above all, by precept and example, he interpreted the teaching of the Gita and taught us to reflect on its sublime message. He became one with the Gita. To many of us indeed, he was a living embodiment of the Gita.

To Gurudev Sadhu Vaswani, the Gita was not just a scripture meant to be recited or memorised: it was a manual of practical wisdom, a guide to daily living. Therefore, he urged us: "You must live the Gita, *be* the Gita!"

This book is dedicated to my beloved Gurudev, with the humble aspiration that the simplicity, profundity and wisdom which he brought to his commentaries on the Gita, may be made accessible to as many seekers – and soldiers, on the battlefield that is life.

— **J. P. Vaswani**

Lead the Wanderer Home!

I wonder how many of you are thinking, even as you open the pages of this book: "Another book on the Gita...Why do we have so many of them?"

May I say to you, in all humility, we need many more of them.

Great thinkers, saints and sages have described the Gita as India's greatest gift to all humanity. It is, to my mind, not just a textbook of metaphysics or philosophy. It is not just to be studied or memorised; not used merely to support this or that theory. It is a song of life, a song of creative wisdom. It is a book that can offer each and every one of us the inspiration that we so badly need to make our work and life meaningful.

We can afford to discard many libraries of reference books; indeed, I believe this is already happening, with people turning away from the libraries to seek wisdom on the internet. We can do away with many books, I repeat: but this is a book which all of us must return to, again and again.

Every single *sloka,* indeed every line, every word of the Gita unveils such profound truths and deep spiritual vistas, that books and commentaries have been written on single chapters of the Gita, single concepts from the Gita – nay, single lines of the Gita.

Know thyself, is the call of philosophy. Experience is the beginning of philosophy. Freedom is the goal of philosophy. Life is an exercise in practical philosophy. This is the aspect of the Gita's teaching that I wish to bring out in this little book.

The world is in turmoil today. We are like lost children, just being swept along with the tide of events that are overtaking us, at a pace that we cannot control. We seem to have lost control over ourselves and our lives. All of us must pass through a period of loneliness and internal conflict before we can enter into self-knowledge and assume mastery over the self and the life we lead here. It is essential for us to realise, that in this struggle for self-knowledge and self-mastery, we are not alone.

Arjuna the great hero, Arjuna, the brave warrior, stands confounded and lonely on the field of Kurukshetra.

> My limbs fail, my mouth is parched, my body quivers, my hair stands on end. My Gandiva bow slips from my hand and my skin burns all over; I am not able to stand steady; my brain is reeling. [I:29-30]

Arjuna is sad and lonely. His mind is agitated; his consciousness is clouded. This hero of a hundred fights, suddenly begins to suffer from nervous fright.

Sounds familiar to all of us, doesn't it? We have felt likewise, haven't we all?

This has happened to men and women again and again. Escape, renunciation, turning our back on life and action, running away from it all, seems a very easy option. What am I going to achieve by struggling, we think, giving into despair and pessimism. What is the purpose, what is the meaning to this struggle called life?

> I desire not victory, O Krishna, nor Kingdom, nor pleasures. What is Kingdom to us, O Krishna, or enjoyment or even life itself? [I:32]

Truly has it been said, by innumerable commentators, that the 'battle' here is not a fight between armies, but a war within a soul. They tell us that the chariot which stands amidst the raging armies symbolises the body, in which the mind (Arjuna) is seated, along with Sri Krishna, the *Atman,* the Self. The horses symbolise the five senses. And Kurukshetra is the plane of action, the plane of friction, the world of strife and contradictions that we inhabit. Therefore, have the wise ones taught us that life on earth is a battle, and all of us must fight the good fight, for the just cause.

It was Swami Ramdas who said, "There is no greater victory in the life of a human being than victory over the mind: The true soldier is he who fights not the external, but the internal foes."

Fortunately for us, as for Arjuna, Sri Krishna holds the reins of the chariot – for God is always on man's side in all the struggles of a virtuous life. So when Arjuna says, "I will not fight," and sinks into silence and despair, Sri Krishna is at hand to guide him with words of wisdom. "Weep not," the Master tells His dear, devoted disciple, "but be a man, a master-man! Abandon weakness! Stand up in courage! Stand up and fight!"

Gurudev Sadhu Vaswani emphasised the heroic note in the Gita. He called the Gita, the "Song of Strength", the "Song of *shakti*". This is the strength, this is the vital *shakti,* to which I wish to draw everyone of you!

Uttishta! Paramtapa! Stand up, Arjuna!

Each one of us is called upon to fulfill our tasks in life. To fight the good fight, as I have said repeatedly. Evil is within us, evil is outside us. Everywhere, there are wrongs to be righted, weaknesses to be fought and conquered – within, without. We cannot say, "I will not fight!"

The Lord tells us, even as He tells Arjuna: "Stand up and fight! For life is a battlefield."

Stand up and fight evil! Stand up and fight injustice! Conquer the ego! Vanquish your weaknesses! Conquer the self! Make your life worthwhile and meaningful! Discover the truth about yourself – that you are not the material, physical body that you wear, but the immortal *Atman* within! Discover your Homeland, and the special link, the invisible silken bond that ties you with the Supreme One, the Oversoul!

The message of the Gita is the message of courage, heroism and *Atma shakti.* The Gita teaches us that weakness is a sin, while *shakti* is a spiritual virtue. The Gita inspires us to victory — moral and spiritual — in the battle of life.

The Gita's universal relevance and timeless appeal are emphasised by its total avoidance of dogma and bigotry; and so Sri Krishna tells us:

> However men approach Me, even so I greet them. For the path men take from every side is Mine, O Arjuna!   [IV:11]

What I hope to do through the pages of this book is stated simply. I would like each and every one of you to read the Gita; reflect on it; interpret it in the light of your own life and experience; and translate all that you have learnt into deeds of daily living. The Gita is first and foremost a dynamic scripture, a scripture of action and life.

For those of us who aspire to a life beyond this worldly life, it has more to offer, the promise of liberation, freedom, *mukti* from the cycle of birth and death.

The Bhagavad Gita, literally, The Song of The Lord, is essentially a song of the Life of the Spirit. It shows us how the *jivatma*, the individual, who lives the life of suffering, misery and separation here on earth, may be united with his Divine Source, the *Paramatma*. It shows us the Path which we must take to reach our Homeland. But this way is to be trodden, not merely spoken about. Step by step must every being move on the Path, until the wanderer reaches his true Home!

The Gita in Context

The Mahabharata is greater in size of the two great epics of India. Scholars tell us that it is more than eight times the size of Homer's Iliad and Odyssey put together. It contains over 100,000 stanzas, and is therefore called *Satasahasri*. It consists of 18 *Parvas* or chapters, with a 19th section which forms a sort of appendix to the whole. It is the world's longest poem, and its unique feature is that it contains within itself, the Bhagavad Gita which is the ultimate world scripture.

Written by Rishi Ved Vyasa who is thought to have compiled the *Vedas*, the Mahabharata is often referred to as the fifth *Veda*, for its myriad stories and incidents bring out every truth that is embedded in the *Vedas*. *Yata Dharma Stato Jaya* – where there is righteousness, there is victory – may be said to be the central theme of this encyclopaedic epic. It celebrates the ultimate and unfailing triumph of good over evil, and the story brings home to us eternal, universal truths that can teach us to aspire to the best life here and hereafter. Rishi Ved Vyasa tells us:

Yadihaasti tadanyatra
Yannehaasti na kutrachit

That which is here can be seen elsewhe. but that which is not found here, cannot be seen anywhere else.

The Kurukshetra war occurs as the climax of the great epic. As losers in the game of dice masterminded by the evil Shakuni, the Pandavas are exiled from their Kingdom, having lost everything they possess to the Kauravas. They are forced to spend twelve years in the forest, and the thirteenth year incognito, before they can reclaim their lost Kingdom. Having paid the full penalty, after thirteen long years of exile, they come back to claim their lost Kingdom.

Acting as their emissary, Sri Krishna goes to the Kauravas and demands that the Pandavas' Kingdom should be returned to them forthwith. This request is refused outright by Duryodhana.

Yudhishtira, ever ready to make a compromise in the interests of peace, asks for just five villages in lieu of their Kingdom. But the adamant Duryodhana pays no heed to the plea. Now, a battle becomes the only option by which the dispute can be settled.

Thus, the stage is set for the battle between the Pandavas and Kauravas at Kurukshetra. Kings and their armies from all over the land join one of the camps and participate in the ensuing battle. Though Sri Krishna does not take sides or fight in the battle, He graciously consents to become Arjuna's charioteer. Bhishma is declared the Chief of the Kauravas, while Draupadi's brother Drishtadhyumna, is chosen to be the leader of the Pandava army.

As the gongs are sounded and conches blown to signal the start of the war, Arjuna falls into deep distress and despair at the sight of his kinsmen and friends ranged against one another, ready to kill and be killed, for the sake of the land. He lays down his bow and declares that he cannot fight such a ruthless battle.

At this juncture, Sri Krishna, acting as his true friend, guide and guardian, counsels him on his duty, and on the ideal attitude to life and action that a man should adopt. It is this advice which is enshrined in the Bhagavad Gita, which many of us revere today as the ultimate scripture.

The Gita is but a section, a part of the great epic Mahabharata. But it is the very core of the great epic, and is one of the most authoritative texts of Hindu values and principles. The context of the world's greatest epic fades into insignificance when one considers the universality of its teaching.

The Significance of the Gita for the Twenty-first Century

Dharmakshetre Kurukshetre Samaveta Yuyutsavaha...

Let us note, the very first word of the Gita is the word *'dharma'*.

On the holy plain, the field of righteousness, the field of the Kurus, the Kurus have gathered together, eager for battle.

The opening word of this magnificent scripture is *dharma,* the great word of ancient India. Just as beauty was dear to Greece and power was dear to Rome, *dharma* was close to the soul of India. Our ancient *rishis* exhorted us to 'build our life in *dharma'*.

Dharma is derived from *dhru* which means 'hold'. *Dharma* is the power, the force, the *jivan shakti* which holds life. *Kshetra* means 'field'. Let us therefore, ask ourselves: "What am I sowing in the field of life, *dharma* or *adharma?*" If you are one of the blessed souls who are sowing the seeds of *dharma,* your life becomes a song, a Gita of the Lord!

In this *Kaliyuga,* which is characterised by the degeneration of *dharma,* it becomes imperative for each of us, as individuals, to adhere to *dharma* in the measure that is possible to us. And, it is my firm conviction that the Gita can be our leading light, our beacon of hope in this endeavour.

I believe too, that it is necessary and desirable for all Indians, especially the youth, professionals and young parents to cultivate familiarity with this precious scripture which is our great heritage. Knowing the essence of its teachings and putting into practise its practical precepts is the best way of escaping the dominant dark forces of this age.

At this juncture, I must add it is not the purpose of this book to offer a new commentary on the Gita, or indeed to give detailed explanations of the chapters or the *slokas*. This is an arduous task which has been accomplished with great success by our saints, sages and spiritual teachers. Sri Adi Shankara himself wrote one of the most respected and authoritative commentaries on the Gita. Other distinguished spiritual luminaries like Sri Ramanuja, Sri Madhavacharya, Sri Vallabhacharya and Sri Jnaneshwar have added valuable insights to their respective *bhashyas*. In modern times Lokmanya Tilak, Mahatma Gandhi and Sri Aurobindo have written on the Gita. As for me, I was privileged to be the disciple of a great-souled saint, whom many regarded as a "living Gita" – Gurudev Sadhu Vaswani. This book draws greatly on his extensive teachings, discourses and writings on the Gita.

What I wish to offer to my readers through the pages of this book is a practical guide to a *dharmic* life based on the Gita. The Gita is the core strength of every Hindu – indeed, the universal guide to every thinking, sensitive human being who realises that life does not stop at the physical and material level. Arjuna too, was swayed by the claims of the material world; he was deceived by his worldly attachments; he failed to perform his duty. He was overwhelmed by the choices before him. He could not take a decision knowing that it would be just and right and ethical. All he wanted was to give up, quit, turn away from action and sink into the lethargy of inaction.

Sounds very familiar, doesn't it? It has happened to all of us at one time or another.

We too, are faced with multiple problems; we too, face suffering and pain; we too, are impelled to give it all up and escape into inaction and oblivion. The Gita can help us face life's challenges bravely, positively. It can help us to come to terms with ourselves and the meaning of our life. It can help us stand up and face life's complexities and emerge victorious in the internal conflict that rages permanently within us.

The message of the Gita is affirmative; the message of the Gita is dynamic. It is a message that we all need to affirm and internalise in our daily lives. This is what I hope to pass on to you in the following pages.

A Word Before we Begin to Read about the Gita

All devout Hindus believe that the Gita was uttered by Sri Krishna, the Almighty Lord Himself, for our benefit. Arjuna and his dilemma were the pretext for the Lord to address those issues which He felt would be important for all of us to know. The Gitopadesh is for each and every one of us: it addresses the vital question of our liberation or *moksha,* and unveils the ultimate secret which is the *saranagati tattva,* the profound philosophy of absolute surrender to the Lord.

Who has given us the best translation of the Gita? Which is the best commentary on the Gita? These are questions that must not detain us. My friends who constantly 'surf the net' as they call it, tell me that devout, cultured, pious men and women have actually come to exchange verbal blows on each other over their favoured translations and commentators. I do not propose to enter into these questions. As I have already made clear to you, my foremost source for this book is Gurudev Sadhu Vaswani's commentary and translation. However, we are blessed to have available before us, the commentaries of great souls who have toiled to make the Gita accessible to all of us. I bow in deep devotion before all these great souls and offer you the insights I have gathered from them all.

Chapter - 1

Arjuna Vishada Yoga

It is significant that the very first chapter of the Gita is entitled "The Yoga of the Depression of Arjuna".

Perhaps the very first step on the path of spirituality for many seekers is depression, darkness of the soul. Our greatest saints and sages have gone through this period of loneliness, wandering and quest. What is the meaning of life? Why are we born here upon this earth? Where do we go from here?

We must all pass through this period of questioning, this period of search, this period of loneliness and despair before we enter into *atma sakshaatkara* or self-knowledge. How can we hope to realise God if we do not realise our true nature? Arjuna enters this phase of darkness in order to cross over into true knowledge, the knowledge, of the self and the knowledge of *Brahman*.

What happens in this chapter

The Gita begins with the sound of hundreds of conches and battle drums. These are stirring sounds of a great impending battle, a battle for inner victory. But one soul is afraid to enter the battle lines; it is ready to give up the struggle — for it is afraid of death, the death of its passions and desires. Perhaps it also fears the death of the body, for death seems to be the end of everything.

As we saw, the despondency, the depression or the loneliness of Arjuna is the starting point of the Gita. It is significant that the very first chapter of the Gita begins with *Vishada Yoga,* a deep depression, the dark night of the soul. Arjuna's heroism and courage crumble, giving way to utter confusion and despair. How can he participate in the terrible carnage that is about to ensue? How can he take up arms against his own kinsmen and elders, grandfathers, teachers, grandsons, cousins, uncles and friends? How could he set out to destroy his own relatives and friends for the sake of a Kingdom? Can there be any pleasure in kingship that is obtained at such a terrible price? Is it not wisdom to turn away from such a terrible sin that will destroy all the ancient traditions of the family? Surely, the better option would be for himself (Arjuna) to be unresisting and unarmed, allowing the enemies, the sons of Dhritarashtra, to slay him.

Seeing the armies arrayed at Kurukshetra, Arjuna's question to Sri Krishna is this: "How can I fight those whom I love?" Indeed, it may be said that this opening chapter is largely in the questioning or interrogatory mode. As Arjuna sees the situation, his spiritual dilemma intensifies. His inner predicament assumes terrible proportions. He marshals several arguments – social, ethical, moral and spiritual, to state that the ensuing war would be a terrible act of sin, and informs Sri Krishna that he will not fight in such a war.

Arjuna is indeed sincere, but his mind is under a cloud. His words are uttered in agony and attachment (*moha*). He has yet to learn the lesson of desireless action. His *vairagya* is not true determination, it is born out of illusion and attachment. He says, "I will not fight," and sinks into silence.

Having spoken thus, on the battlefield, Arjuna sank down on his chariot-seat, casting away his bow and arrow, his mind overwhelmed by grief.   [I:47]

And so, Arjuna the great hero, Arjuna, the brave warrior, stands confounded on the field of Kurukshetra.

My limbs fail, my mouth is parched, my body quivers, my hair stands on end. My Gandiva bow slips from my hand and my skin burns all over; I am not able to stand steady; my brain is reeling.   [I:29-30]

Arjuna is sad and lonely. His mind is agitated; his consciousness is clouded. This hero of a hundred fights, suddenly begins to suffer from nervous fright.

This has happened to men and women again and again. Renunciation, turning our back on life and action, running away from it all, seems a very easy option. In Arjuna's case, he is moved to pity, and pity opens the door to weakness. "Can I slay my kinsmen and be happy?" he asks.

I desire not victory, O Krishna, nor Kingdom, nor pleasures. What is Kingdom to us, O Krishna, or enjoyment or even life itself?   [I:32]

Arjuna is no coward; nor is he foolish, unwise. From social, ethical as well as the narrow worldly point of view, he marshalls his arguments to prove that the battle he is about to fight is not really worthwhile.

Arjuna is not suffering from momentary weakness or fear. He is in fact passing through a deep spiritual crisis caused by the realisation that the social, moral, religious and ethical values that he had always cherished as precious and dear to his heart, are suddenly crumbling down all around him. The fundamental principles of his life are challenged by the disturbing reality of the situation he finds himself in.

Such a crisis can come to only noble souls. The unthinking, insensitive, average person does not face such despair or indecision. It only happens to a person whose faith in his values is threatened.

Compassion, *daya,* is indeed a commendable virtue. So is renunciation, *tyaga.* But there are occasions when it is inappropriate. Arjuna is a *kshatriya,* and his *swadharma* is to engage in righteous war. But he is overcome by attachment and falls into confusion. Not only does he reject his duty, he is ready to renounce all action for the sake of those people who are dear to him: his *acharya,* his grandfather, his kinsmen and former friends. "I will not fight," he tells Sri Krishna, "Let them kill me." The Gandiva slips from his hand, and he sinks into utter despair.

Can a surgeon refuse to wield his surgical knife out of compassion for the patient?

Can a police officer let a criminal escape out of compassion for a fellow human being?

And let us remind ourselves too, that Prahlada renounced his own father, but that was to remain steadfast and loyal to Hari, his beloved Lord!

There are renunciations and renunciations. There is our duty; there is our discrimination. The question is when it is time to take a call and decide on the course of action we must follow.

What shall we do? Renounce action, give up on our duty and choose a 'superior' path as it seems to us?

We must remember too, Arjuna's despair is no ordinary despair, it is not for nothing that it is called *Vishada Yoga* – or the *yoga* of despair. To feel such acute despair is also a step in the process of *yogic* achievement. It is not a state of *tamas,* slothful inaction, leading to utter frustration. It is the *yoga* of despondency which develops into a deep spiritual quest for the truth. It is an awakening of the consciousness that the mind must evolve beyond its narrow confines and expand its consciousness.

Again and again, on the battlefield of our life, we will find ourselves in the same situation as Arjuna. The Lord may not be with us in person, but His grace and mercy are ever abiding in our lives. If we surrender ourselves at His Lotus Feet, He is sure to show us the way, even as He guided Arjuna out of despair.

For Your Reflection

Tagore's story "The Renunciation" tells us about a young couple, Hemanta and Kusum, who have fallen in love and married each other. Hemanta adores Kusum, but Kusum becomes moody and dejected after the wedding. Soon Hemanta finds out that Kusum is not, like him, a brahmin by birth, but the orphaned daughter of a low-caste family. When Hemanta's father, Harihar, hears this, he orders Hemanta to throw his wife out of their home.

Hemanta confronts Pyare Mohan, the old man who, as a foster-father and guardian to Kusum, had arranged this wedding, and asks him why he had hidden the truth about Kusum from his family. Pyare Mohan replies that he had old scores to settle with Hemanta's father Harihar, and chose to trick him in this manner.

"I shall have to throw Kusum out of my house now," Hemanta says to him. "It is my kula dharma.

I cannot permit the defiling of my caste. Will you look after her when I abandon her?"

"I thought it would be doing a good turn to get her married to you since you loved each other," says the old man. "Why should I take up her responsibility now? It is not my business to protect all wives abandoned by their husbands."

Hemanta returns home, his mind in a great turmoil. Kusum is waiting for him, utterly desolate and bereft. She falls at his feet silently and sheds bitter tears of sorrow. Hemanta's heart melts at the sight of his beloved wife in such misery.

The father arrives outside their room and tells Hemanta, "Enough is enough. Turn her out now."

Hemanta makes up his mind. "Father," he says firmly, "I cannot forsake my wife."

"Would you lose your caste?" roars the father in anger.

"I do not care for it," Hemanta replies.

"In that case, I renounce you!" cries the father.

Questions:

1. Was Hemanta right to stick by his wife?

2. What was his duty under the circumstances?

3. What is your reaction to his father's 'renunciation'?

4. What other course of action, do you think, was open to Hemanta?

Exercises:

What do you understand by duty?

1) fulfilling your obligations; 2) following your conscience; 3) doing your allotted work or 4) doing whatever needs to be done?

Put down what you perceive to be your duty or *swadharma*. (As a student, as a worker, as an employer, as a mother/father/spouse/child.)

Under what circumstances would you be justified in turning your back upon your duty?

Chapter - II

Sankhya Yoga

The second chapter is entitled "The Yoga of Knowledge". If we are talking about *atma sakshaatkara* or self-knowledge, the most essential knowledge that we need is this: that this physical existence that we live is only superficial; that the physical body we wear is only a garment. The reality behind the body is the *Atman*, the eternal spirit.

What happens in this chapter

With this Chapter, the Lord's teaching begins. The Lord tries to stir Arjuna out of his sudden faint-heartedness by appealing to his reason and his intelligence. Until now, He has listened to Arjuna in silence, allowing him to express his anguish and agony. Now, it is time for Him to dispel Arjuna's doubts – indeed, to dispel the ignorance of all humanity – with the brilliant message of the Gita.

It would be fair to say that the great spiritual truths revealed in this chapter form as it were, the foundation on which the Gita's teachings are built. While the Lord enunciates very profound and therefore somewhat difficult concepts, He allows Arjuna to interrupt Him several times with his questions and his doubts, so that he may be convinced by the teachings. Thus, the Lord proves to be a wonderful teacher.

Three great truths are declared in this Chapter:

1. The *Atman*, the Real, is deathless. It cannot be destroyed. Death is an experience, not of the *Atman,* but of the body.

2. The body is subject to change, disease, old

age and death. It has to be cast off like a worn-out garment, so that the *Atman* may assume other embodiments. For death is certain for the born, as is birth for the dead. Thus grieving over death is futile.

3. The enlightened aspirant must realise that his right is to work, and work alone. The fruits, the results of the work should never be his concern.

Feelings, thoughts, perceptions, emotions, will power, intelligence, discrimination, these are but functions of the physical human body. The soul transcends these functions, and is above and beyond all that we think, feel and desire.

And where is this soul? It is not 'located' in any particular corner or seat of the body. It pervades the whole.

Arjuna has spoken with deep feeling. But he has not spoken with true wisdom. He has identified himself, his kinsmen and his enemies, with the bodies they wear. He thinks that the joys and sorrows of the body are the joys and sorrows of man. The soul is not the body and the ego; the body and the ego will change and eventually pass away. The *Atman* will persist and abide.

When we rise above the senses, above the duality of pleasure and pain, when we cease to desire anything, when we do not expect anything, we will experience true peace and contentment. The man who realises that he is but an instrument of God, acts dispassionately, desirelessly. Such a one is the *stithaprajna*, the man of steady wisdom.

> He whose mind is free from anxiety amid pains, indifferent amidst pleasures, loosened from passion, fear and rage, he is called a seer illumined. [II:56]

Such a man of stable mind conquers the senses, the passions and emotions, attains to true peace. He becomes one with *Brahman.*

> This is the Divine state (*brahmistithi*), O Arjuna! Having attained thereto, none is ever bewildered. Whoso, even at the end (the hour of death), is established in that state, he goeth to *brahma-nirvana*, the bliss of God. [II:72]

The Nature of the *Atman* according to the Gita:

The soul, or *Atman,* is indestructible and eternal. Contrary to what Arjuna thinks, he cannot kill Bhishmacharya. The *Atman* neither slays nor can it be slain. It is never born, never dies and never ceases to be. It is *nitya* (eternal), *sasvatah* (permanent) and *purana* (very ancient). When the body dies, the *Atman* does not cease to be; it just leaves the body and enters into a new one. Weapons cannot cleave it, fire cannot burn it, water cannot moisten it and wind cannot dry it. It is impenetrable, incombustible, all pervading, stable, immobile, invisible, imperceptible and immutable.

The word 'death' as we use it in the worldly sense, is nothing but the departure of the *Atman* from one body to enter into another. Nor is it wise to grieve over the death of the body; for this human body is constituted by the five elements. It is but the abode of the eternal *Atman* to experience the fruits of its *karmas*. When these *karmas* are exhausted, the physical body has no reason to continue its existence. It drops down.

Having understood the true nature of the *Atman,* we must learn to perform all our actions upon this earth in the right spirit of *nishkama karma*, desireless action. It is important to note that we should only renounce/detach ourselves from the fruits of the actions; and NOT from the actions themselves.

The highest duty of a *kshatriya* like Arjuna is

to fight a just war. Arjuna should therefore set aside the result of the war, victory or defeat, and just do his duty by fighting the war. By so doing, he is not just performing an action; he is doing *karma yoga,* which will eventually lead him on to *mukti* or liberation.

For Your Reflection

The following story was narrated by Sri Ramana Maharishi in the course of a discussion on the nature of the Atman.

The Sage Ribhu had taken great efforts to teach his disciples the ultimate Truth of the One without a second, and the true nature of the Atman. However, one of his disciples, Nidagha, despite his sincerity and devotion, just could not progress on the path of self-knowledge. He completed his gurukula stay and settled down in his native place to lead a life devoted to prayer and piety.

But the Sage Ribhu loved his disciple as deeply as the latter venerated his Master. In spite of his age, Ribhu would often go to visit his disciple in the town, just to see how far the latter was progressing on the path of self-knowledge. Oftentimes, he would go in disguise, so that he might observe Nidagha in action, unaware that he was being watched.

On one such occasion Ribhu, who had put on the disguise of a village rustic, found Nidagha amidst an eager crowd of onlookers, who had gathered to watch the passing of a royal procession. Unrecognised by the town-dweller Nidagha, the village 'rustic' enquired what the bustle was all about, and was told that the King was going in the procession.

"Oh! Is it really the King? Is he going in the procession? But where is he? Please show him to me!" said the excited rustic.

"There he is, on the elephant," said Nidagha. "You can't miss him. He is right in the middle of the procession, riding on the elephant!"

"You say the King is on the elephant. Yes, I see the two," said the rustic, "but which is the King and which is the elephant?"

"What!" exclaimed Nidagha. "You see the two, but do not know that the man above is the King and the animal below is the elephant? What is the use of talking to a man like you?"

"Pray, be not impatient with an ignorant man like me," begged the rustic. "But you said above and below, what do they mean?"

Nidagha could not take it any more. "You see the King and the elephant, the one above and the other below. Yet you want to know what is meant by 'above' and 'below' he burst out. "If things seen and words spoken can convey so little to you, action alone can teach you. Bend forward, and you will know it all too well."

The rustic bent down obediently. Nidagha got on his shoulders and said: "Know it now. I am above as the King, you are below as the elephant. Is that clear enough?"

"No, not yet," was the rustic's gentle reply. "You say you are above like the King, and I am below like the elephant. The 'King', the 'elephant', 'above' and 'below', so far it is clear. But pray, tell me what you mean by 'I' and 'you'!"

When Nidagha was thus confronted all of a sudden with the mighty problem of defining a 'you' apart from an 'I', light dawned on his mind. At once he jumped down and fell at his Master's feet saying: "Who else but my venerable Master, Ribhu, could have thus drawn my mind from the superficialities of physical existence to the true Being of the Self? Oh! Gracious Master, I crave Thy blessings."

Exercises:

There is just one important question which you must try to answer: Please ask yourself this simple question: Who am I?

Chances are, you may have multiple answers to this question. Put them all down.

Who are you? You might begin by answering – "I am Ram/Rahim/Robert." But if the question persists,

you might add, "I'm a teacher/doctor/scientist/
businessman."

You might take it further, "I'm so and so's
father/husband/son/neighbour." You may add, with
a trace of pride, "I'm a rich man/a millionaire/an
industrialist/a minister."

Mothers may add, with motherly affection, "I'm
Chintu's/Bunty's/Nikki's mother."

Some of you may say, "I'm the President/
Secretary of the Chamber of Commerce."

But beyond all this – who are you?

"I'm a good human being," some of you may be
able to assert, quite truthfully.

Which is all very well, but the truth is that all
these answers are incomplete. They reveal that you
really do not know yourself.

This might irritate you. You may protest, "Of
course I know myself. How can you or any one else
tell me something that I don't know about myself?"

The truth is, we are all in ignorance of our true
nature. We identify ourselves with the body, with a
physical form, which is smaller than a speck of dust
in the infinite vastness of the cosmos. We identify

with our profession and social status, which is about as insignificant as a fly on the windowpane.

Ask yourself, "Who am I?" Look for the answer in the heart within. "Where do I come from? Why am I here? What is the purpose of this existence of mine?" You will be led to the truth that you are not the body you wear!

My friends, I urge you to become aware of the value of this human birth. It is priceless! It has been bestowed upon each one of us for a specific purpose, that we may realise what we are, whence we came, and wither we are to return.

We are not the bodies that we wear. We are immortal spirits. We are not this; we are *That!*

Everyday, as you wake up in the morning, I urge you to repeat this *mahavakya* given to us by the rishis of our ancient land, *Tat Twamasi! That Thou art!* Thou art not this, the body, that thou take thyself to be. Thou art the immortal soul! This is the very first commandment of the Bhagavad Gita – thou shalt never, never identify thyself with the body!

Are you afraid to die? Are you afraid of losing your loved ones to death? What is death? What do you imagine will happen to you after death?

Perhaps the greatest gift we gain when we cease to identify with the body, is freedom from the fear of death.

The fact is, as the Gita tells us, there is no death for the soul, for it was never born, and it will never die. Perhaps this is the reason why, in our subconscious mind, we refuse to accept the fact of death! When you realise that you are not the body, fear of death is dismissed, as a fear born of ignorance.

If you would progress on the path of self-realisation, you must stop identifying yourself with the body. You must move away from the "shoes" you wear. This is indeed the significance of the custom practised by Hindus, removing one's shoes before one enters a temple or a holy place. This is symbolic of the idea that we move away from body-consciousness to walk upon the sanctified ground, which will help us move towards God-realisation.

We cannot cast off the body, literally. But we can change our perspective by dwelling on the idea that we are not the bodies we wear, we are the immortal spirits within. This makes a tremendous change in the outlook.

The human birth has invested us with a body-mind complex; but the body-mind are just instruments to aid our existence here; the truth is the indwelling spirit.

How far are you swayed by external appearances?

Whom would you respect and revere and welcome to your house, a man who arrives in a Mercedes Benz? A man who arrives on a two wheeler or a man who walks in simply?

How much importance do you attach to people's appearance, the clothes they wear and the accessories/jewels they wear on their person?

If you give truthful answers to these questions, you will know how far you have progressed on the path of self-knowledge.

Chapter - III

Karma Yoga

Karma Yoga may be described as the Path of Action.

In the Second Chapter, Sri Krishna had actually suggested that *Karma Yoga* can help us to get the mind under control, as a requisite step to our proceeding on the path of *Gnana Yoga* or the Path of Knowledge. This raises the question: if one is actually competent to walk the path of *gnana*, why should he take trouble with *karma*, action?

The answer to this question is that the fruits of *gnana* cannot be realised until one has mastered the *Karma Yoga*. The body, mind and the *antah karna* or inner instrument are all purified by *Karma Yoga*. All sins are cleansed.

Action, *karma,* is inevitable to human life. Inactivity is physically impossible: even the mere maintenance of the body is not possible without action. Avoiding action does not automatically lead to perfection.

What is essential is that we perform right action, avoiding both *akarma* (inaction) and *vikarma* (wrong action).

Right action is of three kinds: 1) *Dharma* or duty; 2) *Lokasangraha* or the well being of the world; and 3) *Yagna* or sacrifice.

These *karmas* help us rise above *moha* (desire) *raga* (attraction) and *dwesha* (hatred). The way out of *vikarma* is the way of self-surrender, the way of surrendering the fruits of our actions as a *yagna* (sacrifice) to the Lord.

Thus, is Sri Krishna's doctrine of action unfolded in this chapter.

What happens in this chapter

This chapter outlines for us the Path of Action.

Arjuna is thrilled by the picture of the illumined *stitaprajna,* and wants to know why he should take up any action at all, when the superior way of knowledge or *gnana* is open to him.

In answer to Arjuna's query, Sri Krishna unfolds His doctrine of action. The ideal of *Karma Yoga* is desireless action. This state cannot be reached by giving up all action. What is demanded is not renunciation of work, but renunciation of selfish desire.

Action, *karma* is inevitable. Inactivity is physically impossible: even the mere maintenance of the body requires action. But the sad fact is that the world is in bondage to work. Therefore, work must be done as *yagna,* an offering to the Lord. This is *nishkama karma* at its best, action as worship of God.

No work is incumbent upon the Lord, yet He continually works, so that He may inspire us by His own example.

Surrendering all actions unto Me, with thy thoughts resting on the Self Supreme, from desire and egoism freed, and of (mental) fever cured, fight thou, O Arjuna! [III:30]

The Lord insists that we must act. Arjuna must fight, for it is his duty as a warrior.

Better is one's own duty (or path or law, *swadharma*), though imperfectly done, than the duty of another, well discharged. Better death in (the discharge of) one's own duty. To follow another's duty is fraught with danger. [III:35]

Surrender everything to God, and act in a spirit of non-attachment, even like the *Raja yogi,* King Janaka. Act! For without action, life will fail, the Lord urges us.

Thus knowing Him (the Self) as greater than the *buddhi*, steadying the (lower) self by the Self, slay, O Arjuna, the enemy in the form of desire, so difficult to overcome. [III:43]

Think About it...

As Sri Krishna unfolds His doctrine of *Karma Yoga*, the doctrine of action, the doctrine of work, the very first thing He emphasises is devotion to duty. Devotion to one's duty is what the Gita calls *swadharma*. Each one of us has his duties, his obligations to fulfill. My duties may be 'high' or 'low'. It may be someone's duty to govern the nation; it may be another's duty to manage billions of dollars worth of finances and investments; it may be your duty to teach a nursery class; it may be your friend's duty to tend a garden; it may be my duty to run an office efficiently; it may be my duty to sweep the roads clean.

The Master is careful to point out to us that it is not *what* we do that matters; it is the *way* we do it that matters.

Karma Yoga has been described as the *yoga* of heroism. It entails that we give up selfishness, which is very difficult to achieve. According to *Karma Yoga,* spiritual progress begins with selfless service. What are the main teachings of *Karma Yoga?*

* Plunge yourself into selfless work. Do your duty and a little more. Work for the welfare of others. Selfish work retards spiritual growth; selfless work elevates you to lofty heights of true joy and peace.

* Selflessness grows but gradually! Work patiently and ceaselessly; bear in mind the

splendid examples of the great *Karma Yogis*.

* Grow in the virtues of love and compassion. Put others before yourself.

* Dedicate your work to the Lord. Let your work become a form of worship.

* Develop the spirit of detachment, non-attachment to work and the results of work. Do not be swayed by success and failure, praise and blame. Do not expect rewards, offer your work to the Lord in the spirit of *yagna* or sacrifice.

* One important function of selfless work is that it makes possible the purification of the mind.

* Be calm and unattached. Act with wisdom and understanding, so that you may acquire "skill in action".

* The motive with which you act is the most important aspect of *Karma Yoga*. *Karma Yoga* is performed for the sake of God alone, with the sole aim of realising God. Name, fame, philanthropy, social reform, power, release from sin – all these, when desired as results, detract from *Karma Yoga*. If the motive is pure and selfless, it is *Karma Yoga*. If the motive is impure, it is not.

What are the qualities of a *Karma Yogi?*

* He should be absolutely free from lust, greed, wrath and selfishness.

* He should be detached and desireless.

* He should be humble, free from pride and vanity.

* He should be pure, simple and sweet in his expressions.

* He should have a loving and sociable nature.

* He should be flexible and adaptable by nature.

* He should rejoice in the welfare of others.

* He should exercise self-control over his emotions, actions, his palate, his speech and his senses.

* He should lead a life of simplicity.

* He should work to maintain his body as a temple of the Lord, he should have a sound, strong and healthy body, for in it dwells his eternal *Atman.*

* He should be dispassionate, not swayed by sensual attachments.

* He must possess equanimity, a balanced mind. Insult, injury, disrespect and dishonour do not affect him. Respect, honour, praise and power do not tempt him.

* He is a man of kindness, courtesy and love. All that he does, he does with pure devotion and love of the Lord. For him *lokasangraha* is a form of worship.

* He must conquer the following weaknesses which will hinder his progress:

    1. Ego and irritability;

    2. Self-assertive nature;

    3. Fault-finding with others;

    4. Idle gossip and vain arguments;

    5. Half-hearted efforts; and

    6. Procrastination.

* A true *Karma Yogi* should see the good in all people—and at the same time, make allowances for their weaknesses. Only then will he be worthy of calling himself a true devotee of the Lord.

When it is properly understood and practised, *Karma Yoga* can give the aspirant rapid progress on the path of self-realisation.

For Your Reflection

There is a story in the Mahabharata which emphasises the sanctity attached to one's duty.

A young seeker took to the life of renunciation (sanyas). He lived a life of austerity and penance in the forest, and thus acquired tremendous *taposhakti* (power of *tapasya*). One day, as he was sitting in deep meditation under a tree, a few leaves fell on him, disturbing his concentration. He glanced up at the tree in anger, and saw two birds, a crow and a crane, fighting with each other over their perch on a branch. The moment his angry glance fell on them, they were burnt away by the sheer power of his annoyance, reduced to cinders and ashes before his astonished eyes.

The sanyasi was delighted and impressed by this display of his own power. "I am well on my way towards becoming a great yogi," he thought proudly.

A few days later, he went to a neighbouring village to beg for food, as was his daily custom. He stood at the door of a house and called out, "Mother, give me bhiksha."

A young woman's voice called from inside the house, "Please wait for a while. I am attending to my duty. I will be with you soon."

The sanyasi grew angry at what he considered to be the temerity of this insignificant person — a mere housewife.

"You wretched woman," he thought to himself. "How dare you keep me waiting? Do you know what kind of shakti I possess?"

As if she could read his thoughts, the voice from inside called out, "And, my dear brother, be patient. Don't think too much of yourself. I'm not a crow or a crane!"

The sanyasi was taken aback. Abashed, he waited silently till the woman of the house came out with food. When he saw her, he simply fell at her feet, for to his limited mind, she seemed to possess a far greater shakti than he did: the power of mind-reading, no less.

"Mother," he said to her with great reverence, "tell me how you acquired such a great gift? What are the yogic techniques you practised? What are the austerities you performed? Do enlighten me!"

"My dear brother, I do not know what you are talking about," said the young woman. "I made you wait because I was attending to the needs of my husband who is ill. That is my prime duty now as a housewife. All my life, I have tried my best to do my duty well. At first, I did my duty towards my *parents. Now that I am a married woman, I do my duty as a wife. This is all the yoga that I practise.*

"But doing my duty has helped me to grow in wisdom and understanding. This is why I was able to read your thoughts, and came to know the fate of the crow and the crane."

"Doing your duty — is that all? Can it make you so powerful? I beg you to tell me more!" pleaded the sanyasi.

"There is nothing more that I can say to you," said the housewife. "But if you wish to know more, I suggest you go to the market, where you will find a vyadha. He can teach you something valuable."

The sanyasi's ego raised its ugly head again. "A vyadha?" he said to himself. "What can a vyadha have to teach me?"

A vyadha in those days was regarded as being very low in social status. He was a man who eked out a living as a hunter or a butcher.

Arrogant as he was, the sanyasi was determined to acquire greater shakti, and decided to seek out the vyadha in question. He found him easily in the market place, a big, fat man, bare-chested, cutting up animal carcasses and bargaining with people over the price of the meat.

Disgusted at this sight, the sanyasi thought to himself, "God forbid that I should seek out such a low creature. What can he possibly teach me?"

Just then the vyadha looked up, and saw the sanyasi standing at a distance and staring at him. "Oh, so you are the sanyasi whom the housewife has sent to me!" he exclaimed. "Please sit here until I have finished with my business." The sanyasi did as he was told, while the vyadha attended to his work. After some time, he shut his shop and said to the sanyasi, "Let us go to my house now."

The man's home was a humble thatched hut. Here too, the sanyasi was made to wait outside while the man disappeared. The sanyasi peeped inside the hut and found that the man was attending to his old parents. He washed them, he fed them and made them comfortable. Then he came out and said to his visitor, "Tell me what I can do for you."

"What is the nature of the Self?" asked the sanyasi. "What is the relationship of God and the individual Self? How may one attain liberation?"

Calmly, the vyadha delivered a discourse on Vedanta, which, in the Mahabharata is called the Vyadha *Gita*. The sanyasi was amazed by the depth and insight of his wisdom.

"Why are you trapped in this lowly form and

this filthy occupation?" he exclaimed. "Why are you doing such filthy and degrading work?"

"My dear friend," said the vyadha, "No work is degrading. No duty is filthy. My birth and circumstances have placed me in this position and I do my job to the best of my ability. I have no attachment to this job, I do it well because it is my duty. I also attend to my duty as a son, and try to keep my parents happy. All that I have told you came to me through doing my duty with detachment. Apart from this, I practise no yoga; I have never been to a forest to meditate either. I only do my duty."

Questions:

1. Do you allow your emotions/desires to interfere in your duty?
2. What do you expect to receive for a duty performed well?
3. Do you think you can suspend all action at any time of your life?
4. What do you understand by 'involvement' in your action? Is this good or bad?

Practical Suggestions

How may we grow in the spirit of Karma Yoga, as advocated in the Gita? So let me pass on to you a few practical suggestions:

1. Realise that selfishness is a curse of human life. Selfishness makes us narrow minded, petty and greedy. We confine ourselves to material goals and work only for money and reward.

   Such a narrow vision shuts out the Divine Light of God from our lives. We are restricted into a groove. Our hearts and minds are contracted.

2. Cultivate the quality of selflessness. This is not easy at first. But as we grow in awareness, we will also grow in unselfishness.

Feel your Oneness with the Divine Spirit. Feel your Oneness with all creation. Be aware of your kinship with all the creatures that breathe the breath of life. Above all, draw inspiration from the great *Karma Yogis* who devote their lives for the benefit of humanity.

It has been said you only require 'a little capital' to cultivate selflessness – a little love, a little mercy and a little sympathy. If you start with just a little, they will multiply in good time, and you will prosper in your chosen path of selfless action.

Remember too, that expecting fruits for our actions will only bind us to the wheel of *karma*. We will have to take birth again to enjoy the fruits that disrupts our spiritual progress.

6. Do not be half-hearted in your efforts. Put in your best, give your 100% to the action you are doing. Careless and half-hearted efforts do no good to anyone, least of all to you. How can you offer your actions to the Lord in the spirit of a *Karma Yogi,* when your heart and soul are not in them? Whether you are folding pamphlets, washing dishes, sticking postage stamps or dusting the furniture, do it as best as your can!

Exercises:

Learn to value your work as an opportunity to evolve towards self-realisation.

I may be a humble office assistant in a government department; but if I do my duty sincerely and honestly, faithfully and conscientiously, the portals of perfection would be readily open, as easily open to me, as it is to the highest in the land! For the Lord makes no discrimination on the basis of caste or creed or social status. I may be the lowest of the low; but if I perform my duty to the best of my ability, the Lord will accept my work with loving grace.

For people who grumble, complain and moan all the time, all work is distasteful and unsatisfactory.

we seek. This retards our spiritual progress.

On the other hand, selfless work promotes inner joy and peace. Motivation need not be lacking either for we are seeking the ultimate goal of freedom, liberation.

3. Conquer the lower passions; conquer the ego self within you. Negative emotions like lust, greed, egoism, envy and anger poison the heart and mind. Even a trace of these emotions sully the purity of your character. A *Karma Yogi* should have perfect self-control over his thoughts, words, deeds, appetite and senses. He should not give in to excess or self-indulgence. He should lead a simple life.

4. Learn to be amiable and adaptable. Accommodate yourself to others. Do not develop rigidity about what you can do and what you want to do. The spirit of give-and-take is vital in our social relationships. A true *Karma Yogi* fits in happily into any kind of situation or environment. Trials, difficulties, obstacles and challenges do not deter him. He is always calm and cool and collected.

5. Keep a healthy mind in a healthy body. Without a strong and healthy body and a pure

and vital mind, no one can do his duty well. Take good care of your body – for it must be put to the best possible use as an instrument of God. Take good care of your body – but do not be attached to your body! Do not give in to vanity and pride.

If you so desire, practise *yoga*. Exercise regularly. Take long walks. Enjoy the fresh air and sunshine. Eat good, nourishing, simple food. Maintain personal hygiene.

6. Cultivate the *yogic* quality of equanimity. The Gita tells us: *Samattwam yoga uchyate.* Equanimity is called *yoga*. You must have a balanced mind, whatever be the conditions around you. You must develop a balanced approach to life.

7. Always be loving and courteous in your dealings with others. Do not complain; do not curse; always speak lovingly and gently. Be polite and courteous to everyone you come across. Let not your best behaviour be reserved for the rich and powerful.

What are the weaknesses, obstacles, personal defects that a *Karma Yogi* must overcome? For it is not enough to nurture the intellect while neglecting

those qualities that management experts now call 'soft skills'. Unfortunately our *karmic* residues have left several negative qualities in us, which we must work to overcome.

1. Accept criticism in the right spirit. Let it be the means to make you better in every way. So avoid being irritated by trifles. Accept your own weaknesses and work to eliminate them gradually.

2. Avoid aggression and over-assertion of your own will upon others. Do not seek to dominate others. Do not impose your will, your opinions on others. Appreciate others' concerns, look at problems and issues from their point of view.

3. The tendency towards aggression and self-assertion are controlled when we develop respect and love for others.

4. Do not find fault with others. Learn to see the good in everyone. Appreciate others – and learn from them.

5. Avoid arguments, vain gossip and futile discussions. What are we trying to prove by getting the better of others by verbal gymnastics? This only agitates the mind and

Nothing will ever make them content, and their efforts are doomed to bring them nothing but disappointment.

How may we avoid such disappointment, frustration and dissatisfaction? Sri Krishna has the answer:

> Surrendering all actions unto Me, with thy thoughts resting on the Self Supreme, from desire and egoism freed, and of (mental) fever cured, fight thou, O Arjuna! [III:30]

Let us surrender the fruits of action to the Lord! Let us stop chasing after 'personal satisfaction'; or 'individual happiness'.

Reflect on this prayer:

Kayena vacha manasendriyairva
Buddhyatmana va prakrite swabhavath
Karoomi yadyad sakalam parasmai
Narayanayeti samarpayami

Whatever I do with my mind, body, speech or with other senses of my body, or with my intellect or with my innate natural tendencies, I offer everything to Lord Narayana.

Chapter - IV

Gnana Karma Sannyasa Yoga

Gnana Karma Sannyasa Yoga has been translated as "The *yoga* of renunciation of action in knowledge". Gurudev Sadhu Vaswani called this "The Secret Doctrine". Sri Krishna Himself calls it *"The Imperishable Yoga"* which He has handed down to the appropriate and rightful recipients – Vasvan, the Sun-god, *Manu,* and to the *raja rishis.* The same secret doctrine is now being taught to Arjuna, who is at once a friend and a disciple to the Lord.

This secret doctrine includes the concept of *nishkama karma* (desireless action) that is central to the Gita. We can see why it includes action, renunciation and knowledge *(karma, tyaga and gnana)* all-in-one. It is action-in-inaction; it is living in the world, yet living withdrawn, in detachment. It teaches us to live and work in this world, and yet hold nothing as ours, for ourselves. It emphasises, once again, that the deathless spirit, the *Atman,* is Supreme. It is the basis of all life and all knowledge. To discover the truth about the *Atman* is to know oneself; to know oneself is to take the first step towards understanding God, the Divine Self within each one of us.

What happens in this chapter

If we have ever wondered how and why great saviours of the human race appear amongst us at certain specific times and contexts, if we wonder with Emperor Akbar as to why the Lord should manifest Himself in human incarnations upon this earth, Sri Krishna has the answer to our query:

> Whenever there is a decay of *dharma* (righteousness), O Arjuna, and there is exaltation of *adharma* (unrighteousness), then I project myself.   [IV:7]

Dharma is a very important concept in Hinduism. *Dharma* is right conduct, right mode of behaviour, right observance which holds, sustains life. In its widest sense, it is righteousness that leads us towards God.

The Lord descends among us as an *avatara*, when *dharma* declines. He comes to help and heal, to protect the world, to save sinking humanity.

> For the protection of the good, for the destruction of the wicked, for the sake of establishing righteousness, I come into birth from age to age.   [IV:8]

This is a great truth, a Divine Mystery which we should know, that God comes among us to help us ascend towards Him. We can approach

Him in any way, He will meet us even on that way.

The Lord acts too; but actions stain Him not. His actions are born of grace and compassion. From His example we should learn what kind of actions we should perform, and what kind of actions we must avoid.

What is action? (*Karma*) And what is inaction? (*Akarma*) Even the wise men are herein bewildered. Therefore, I will declare to thee what action is, knowing which thou shalt be delivered from evil.   [IV:16]

It is important that we must avoid *vikarma* or wrong action.

Do not reject action, the Lord tells us. What binds us is not action, but egotism. What binds us is selfishness. Act, but make your action a *yagna,* an offering to the Lord, and you are no longer bound.

Thus, many kinds of sacrifice are spread out before the Eternal, (i.e. they are the means of reaching God). Know thou that all these are born of action. Knowing this thou shalt be free.   [IV:32]

This is spiritual wisdom at its best. It reveals the fact of unity, the unity of all creatures in the

Atman, the Self, the Spirit, in Krishna. This is both Self-realisation and God-realisation.

> And having known this wisdom (*gnana*), thou, O Arjuna, shall not again fall into this confusion. For, by this wisdom, thou wilt see all beings, without exception, in the *Atman* (the Self), and thus in Me!   [IV:35]

Such wisdom or *gnana*, burns up all our accumulated, as well as future *karmas*.

When this synthesis of *gnana* and *karma* (wisdom and action) is achieved, we act in the spirit of sacrifice to God. Then, nothing can bind us.

> Therefore, cleave asunder with the sword of wisdom this doubt in thy heart, born of ignorance, be established in yoga, and stand up, O Arjuna!   [IV:42]

Think About it...

The question arises in our minds, as it came to Arjuna: How can we seek and attain this wisdom?

The answer is simple. Wisdom can be awakened in us by the Wise. They are the *gnanis*, the *tattva darshanahs*, the seers of the essence of life.

Three things are essential to one who seeks such wisdom:

1. Humility or *paniprata.* We cannot become true disciples, or even hope to attain true wisdom without humility.

2. Investigation or *pariprashna.* Diligent seeking, intensive searching is necessary to attain such wisdom.

3. Service or *seva.* This must be offered in all humility and self-abnegation to the *tattva darshanah,* the guru, who can impart this wisdom to us.

It is well worth paying this price to seek true wisdom: for it leads to supreme peace, or *parama shanti.* It helps us cut aside all doubt and lack of faith, with the sword of knowledge. When we have attained such wisdom, actions cannot bind us. We become free.

For Your Reflection

It is told to us in the **Sai Satcharitra** (the biography of Sri Shirdi Sai Baba) that one of his disciples, called Nana Chandorkar, came to discuss with the Master, his reading of Chapter IV of the Gita. Nana was well-versed in Sanskrit, and quite proud of his personal knowledge of the scriptures. He recited Verse 34 of Chapter IV, and commented on its significance.

Tatviddhi Pranipatena Pariprashnena Sevaya Upadekshyanti Te Jnanam Jnanina Stattwadarshinah

Understand the true nature of knowledge by approaching enlightened men. If you prostrate at their feet, serve them and question them with an open and guileless heart, those wise seers of truth will instruct you in that Knowledge.

Baba quietly asked Nana to explain the verse to him. "Tell me, Nana, what is the meaning of this sloka?"

Nana replied: "By making sashtanga namaskar (prostration), questioning the Guru, serving him, we acquire this gnana. When they are pleased with our service, those gnanis who have attained the real knowledge of Brahman, will give us upadesha of the same."

Baba said to him: "I do not want the general sense of the whole stanza. Give me the word-by-word meaning. What is meant by pariprashna?"

Nana replied, almost instantly, "Why, it means asking questions".

"What is the meaning of the word prashna?" Baba persisted.

"Prashna, as I said, is asking questions," repeated Nana.

"How is it that you are giving me the same meaning for both words?" said Baba. "Look at that word pari. Is there any special meaning for the word pari in Sanskrit?"

Nana became a little hesitant now. "I do not know of any other meaning," he admitted sheepishly.

"Alright then," said Baba. "Can you tell me what is the meaning of seva?"

Nana smiled happily and replied, "Why Baba, it is service, the very same service that we are offering to you daily."

Baba nodded. "And is it enough to render such service? Will that get you the wisdom you seek?"

After a pause which had Nana thinking, Baba continued. "In the sloka, suppose we substitute the word 'gnana' with 'agnana', then what meaning does it give?"

Nana was confused. "Forgive me, Baba," he said sheepishly. "I do not understand how to construe it by substituting agnana."

Baba smiled. "Lord Krishna was the greatest Tattwadarshi *himself*," he remarked. "Why do you think he advised Arjuna to prostrate, serve and question other Gnanis?"

"This too, is something I do not understand," confessed Nana.

If truth were to be told, Nana Chandorkar had thought that with his knowledge of Sanskrit and his reading of the Gita and its learned commentaries, he would be able to tell Baba something new, and may be, even impress Baba with his superior understanding. After all, everyone knew that Baba did not understand Sanskrit. But now, he found that he could not give satisfactory answers to Baba's questions, even on one sloka. He felt quite ashamed. He realised then, that however much one might have read, one cannot be equal to a Gnani. His pride disappeared.

Then it was that Baba, in his distinct manner, gave his own answers to the questions that he had put to Nana, as follows:

1. It is necessary to place your questions before the Guru, to clear all your doubts. But this

questioning should not be for testing the Guru or trying to trap him, but to actually learn more and more from him, and to retain, keep in mind what was learnt, and to put it into practice in daily life. The word *Pariprashna* was used deliberately by Sri Krishna, and reported as such by Ved Vyasa. One should question the Guru, in all humility, with the aim of spiritual progress. That is what is meant by *Pariprashna*.

2. *Seva* or service is another thing that this *sloka* emphasises. Service which is rendered at your convenience, whenever you feel like doing it, is not true *seva*. The true disciple feels that his life, limbs, body and mind are not really his own, but means, instruments by which he can offer his service to the Guru. Only people with this basic wisdom can understand the teaching of the *tattva gnana* by a Guru; others cannot understand such superior wisdom. To teach *gnana* to such persons is just *agnana*.

3. However great a Guru may be, some of his close associates and friends may fail to realise his greatness; they take him to be another ordinary human being like themselves. This is

the effect of *Maya*. That was the reason why Lord Krishna advised Arjuna to serve other *tattwadarshis*.

It is only when a *shishya* approaches the Guru with such great respect and humility that he becomes fit to receive true knowledge, which can lead him to freedom from the bondage of life and death.

Questions:

1. Do you think it is necessary to seek true knowledge-over and above the paper qualifications, the know-how for daily living, and all that you have learnt to make your life successful?

2. If you consider such knowledge essential, do you think you can find it on your own, from books or from other sources?

3. What is your view of 'the secret doctrine' unfolded in this chapter? How essential is this to your daily life?

4. We all know what it is to act: we also know that every action brings with it its own rewards and consequences. What does it mean to renounce the fruits of our actions?

Exersises:

The Lord reveals to us that *Gnana Yoga* is incorporated into *Karma Yoga,* when our actions are performed in the right spirit. Such actions can actually lead us to *moksha* or liberation.

A very important aspect of this *gnana* is unfolded to us by the Lord – namely, His *Avatara rahasya:* this indeed, is the mystery of all mysteries, the Eternal birthlessness, the Divinity of His Being. He incarnates again and again, for the benefit of all humanity. The objective of His *Avatara* is threefold: 1) *Paritranaaya sadhunaam* - i.e. the protection of all seekers; 2) *Vinashaya cha dushkritam* - i.e. overthrow of evil and darkness and *adharma;* 3) *Dharma sansthapanarthaya* – i.e. the re-establishment of righteousness.

Awareness of this *Avatara rahasya,* the mystery of the Lord's incarnation, is itself Ultimate Knowledge, that can lead us to Liberation! But mark this, awareness here does not mean intellectual cognisance, but belief held in *Absolute Faith!* How many of us are capable of such Faith?

One who knows the transcendental nature of My appearance and activities does not, upon leaving the body, take his birth again in this material world, but attains My eternal abode, O Arjuna.   [IV:9]

Scholars have described this path as the path of approaching the Ultimate Truth. We can see how the three paths of *Karma, Gnana* and *Bhakti* are blended in this way.

It is significant that in this chapter, the Lord tells us that He is ready to welcome us to His Divine fold, whatever path we choose to take towards Him:

However men may approach Me, even so do I greet them, for the path that men take from every side is Mine, O Arjuna!   [IV:11]

Chapter - V

Karma Sannyasa Yoga

This chapter deals with the Path of Renunciation of Action. Thus far, Sri Krishna has spoken of *Karma Yoga* together with *Sannyasa Yoga*. *Karma Yoga* is action performed, but dedicated to the Lord. *Sannyasa Yoga*, on the other hand, is yoga attained through renunciation. Which is better, Arjuna asks to know: the right performance of action, or renunciation of action? Can the performance of *karma* be an obstacle in the path of one's Liberation?

What happens in this chapter

This chapter opens with Arjuna's query: Should he renounce his *karma* as a warrior and follow the path of *sannyasa*? Or should he follow his *karma* as a *kshatriya* and fight to the finish? He has been unable to distinguish between *sannyasa* as renunciation of action and *Karma Yoga* which is engaging in action without concern or desire for the fruits of the action.

The Lord assures Arjuna that both of these lead to the highest goal of God-realisation – but the *yoga* of action, he says, is superior to the renunciation of action.

What are we to understand by this? For those of us who are still struggling towards attainment, *Karma Yoga* is far better – because desireless action, steadfast dedication to one's duty is the best way to eliminate negative qualities and purify the mind. But when we have evolved and attained to realisation, we will realise that there is no difference between action and renunciation. Thus *Karma Yoga* is like the ladder we use to climb on to the top of a house, but once we have got there, the ladder becomes unnecessary.

It is pointless to take to renunciation, while one is still restless with passions and desires. Action, especially desireless action can purify and still the mind. In the true spirit of *Karma Yoga,* a man performs acts of selfless service, dedicating all action to the Lord – for the Lord is the assimilation of all *yagna* and *tapas* (sacrifice and austerity).

> And having known Me as the Enjoyer of sacrifices and austerities, as the mighty Ruler of all the worlds, as the Lover of all that lives, he (the Sage) goeth to peace.
>
> [V:29]

Think About it...

In this chapter, the Lord actually suggests that *Karma Yoga* can lead to Liberation, faster than *Gnana Yoga*. The differences between the two paths and the unique features of *Karma Yoga* in which the seeds of *gnana* are actually embedded, are clearly explained. The fact of the matter is, *Karma Yoga* recommends itself to ordinary mortals like us because it is easy to practise. All of us are carrying out our worldly duties to the best of our abilities. We only need to change our attitude towards our work to attain the essential *gnana* or knowledge that can lead to Liberation. The path of action, the attitude of *Karma Yoga* is characterised therefore, by both *soukaryam* (ease of practice), and *saigryam* (quick to yield results).

In this chapter, we are given the Lord's portrayal of a man of true renunciation:

1. He is one who neither hates nor covets and is beyond the *dhvandhas* (opposing pairs).

2. He is one who has conquered his mind and senses and has become the self of all beings.

3. He is untouched by the *phala* (fruit) of the *karmas* even while he is engaged in performing those *karmas.*

4. He sees, hears, touches, smells, eats, moves, sleeps, breathes and yet he acknowledges, "I am not the doer" *(naiva kinchith karomi).*

5. He performs his *karmas* without attachment.

6. In discarding the fruits of action he attains enduring peace.

Lord Krishna concludes: Such a *yogi* knows Me as His Supreme Master and the Lord of all the Worlds *(Sarva loka Maheswaram)* and as the partaker/enjoyer of all *Yajnas (Bhoktharam Yajnatapasam)* as well as the friend of every being *(Suhrudham Sarvabhuthanam).* Knowing Me this way, the Lord states, this type of *yogi* attains tranquility *(Saanthimrucchathi).*

For Your Reflection

Among the characters in the Ramayana, Bharata is regarded by many scholars as the most devout and loyal, the most humble and the perfect embodiment of virtue. In the villages of the North, the people celebrate an annual festival for the episode of the meeting of Rama and Bharata at Chitrakuta, which they consider the most sanctifying part of the Ramayana epic. In this selfish, materialistic world of ours, Bharata's life and offering to Sri Rama stand out as a beacon of light to seekers on the right path, and symbolise Divinity in man.

When Sri Rama was exiled to the forest for fourteen years, the people of Ayodhya followed Rama in hordes out of the city, claiming that they would go to live with him in the forest. King Dasharatha died of a broken heart, unable to bear the tragic parting from his beloved son. When Bharata returned to Ayodhya, he was horrified to learn what had transpired in his absence. Severely upbraiding his mother for her folly and ill-will, he set out in search of Rama, leading a group of stalwarts from the Court, to persuade Rama to return to Ayodhya and to ascend the throne that rightly belonged to him.

It is not easy for any of us to look at the story of Sri Rama from Bharata's point of view. The most cruel and selfish deed in the epic is perpetrated by Bharata's mother Kaikeyi, who actually imagines that her son would be very pleased with her for managing to secure the throne for him. How little she understands her own son! And how difficult it is for her son to prove to others that he knew nothing of the terrible scheme carried out by his mother for his benefit! All that Bharata could do was to swear that he was innocent, and that he would never, ever dream of taking his beloved brother's rightful place on the throne, for this great-souled kshatriya cared nothing for Kingdom or wealth or power. All he wanted was to bring Sri Rama back to Ayodhya.

But Sri Rama's word had been given to his father. He could not now return to Ayodhya. He assured Bharata that he could rule Ayodhya just as well as any one of the brothers. For his part, Bharata insisted that he would indeed be a substitute for Rama — but not in Ayodhya: rather, he would undertake the stipulated fourteen year exile in the forest, while Rama could return to Ayodhya and rule the Kingdom.

Scholars and commentators describe this beautiful episode as one in which "righteousness struggles with righteousness as to which should be more right".

This impasse is finally solved by Sage Vashishta who tells the younger prince, "O, Bharata, rule the Kingdom under Rama's authority and as his deputy. No blame would attach to you then and Rama's *pledge would also be upheld."* Sri Rama too, urges Bharata to rule the Kingdom in his place.

Bharata says to Rama: *"Brother, you are my father and my God. Your least wish is my dharma. Only, I pray to you, give me your sandals. Your holy padhukas shall reign in Ayodhya till you return. And for fourteen years, during your exile, I shall stay outside the city and discharge the King's duties in your place, paying reverent homage to your sandals. At the end of that period, you must promise me that you will return and accept the Kingship."*

Sri Rama accedes to this loving prayer. He places his feet on the sandals and hands them over to Bharata who prostrates himself on the ground and accepts the sandals and carries them on his head, as a symbol of his deep devotion to his brother.

The sandals are placed on the royal throne of Ayodhya; the keeper of the sandals lives as an ascetic, for the next fourteen years, in the village of Nandigram, outside the city of Ayodhya: for he has vowed that he would not return to live in the city until his brother is back on the throne.

Is this not the law laid down in the Gita, that one should serve the world unselfishly and without attachment, leaving the fruit of one's work at the feet of the Lord? Sri Rama fulfilled his vow to his father and lived in the forest for fourteen years; throughout those fourteen long years, Bharata too did his penance at Nandigram, performing his duty as the deputy of his beloved brother, renouncing all the fruits of his action as a true *gnani* and Karma Yogi.

The *Vaishnava traditions exalt Bharata for his selfless devotion to duty and serene detachment from material desires. For fourteen years, till the return of Rama, Bharata installed Rama's padhukas and administered the kingdom as a devotional exercise in the service of his brother. Can we think of a better example of* karma sannyasa yoga?

Questions:

1. What do you expect as a return for your work/ your duty done at home, at work and in society? Money, praise, appreciation, gratitude, reward or recognition?

2. Think about this carefully: does appreciation or the lack of it affect the quality of your work?

3. Is there anything that you do with utter detachment?

4. How do you think people like policemen, civic officials and beaureaucrats should carry out their tasks? Can you apply the same yardstick to your own work? If your answer is no, then why not?

Think about it...

There is much talk about vocational education today. The word vocation is derived from the Latin root which means "to call". Let our work be a calling! Let our work be a labour of love, something that we love to do, something that we enjoy doing, rather than just a source of monetary benefit. A labour of love leads to life's greatest fulfillment.

When I visit big cities – perhaps this disease has travelled to smaller cities and towns too, I find that people who are assigned any work always ask, "What's in it for me?" or "What do I get for this?" People work only for wages today. They have forgotten what it is to work with joy, what it is to make their work a source of delight. This is why work has become a cause of so much boredom and frustration to many.

In the Bhagavad Gita, which I regard as a Bible of humanity, Lord Krishna expounds His doctrine of *Karma Yoga*. He tells Arjuna: "Remember, to work you have the right, but not to the fruit thereof." You must work; you must put in your best efforts, you must not slacken your endeavours. But you must not be disappointed if you do not get the result you seek.

Perhaps many of you will find this unacceptable. You will ask me, "But what about my just compensation? How can anyone work without wages in this world of growing needs?" So let me tell you – of course work and wages go together. They are two sides of the same coin. Whether you work for wages or otherwise, wages are sure to fall into your lap. I am talking about your attitude to work. It is your attitude that will make your life a success or otherwise. And I feel very strongly that your work should be an expression of your love! Those of us who work only for wages will never experience real joy. And when you love your work, you will find it a joy forever.

Work not for wages! Make your work your worship to the Lord. May your God go with you as you work, and you will find that your life and work are both transformed!

How may we cultivate the spirit of *karma sannyasa yoga* advocated by Sri Krishna in this chapter? How can we learn to renounce the fruit of our actions? Let me show you four ways to achieve this.

1. We must learn to give, give and give without any expectation in return.

There are two kinds of men in this world, those who always give and those who always receive.

It is said that the hand of the giver is always higher than the hand of the receiver. The man who gives is a large-hearted man. The large-hearted man, who believes in giving, is the man who is not attached to his wealth or money. The large-hearted man will keep his needs to the minimum. Whatever he has over and above that, he would give away. If he has four watches, he will keep one for himself and will give away the remaining three to those whose need is greater than his. Gurudev Sadhu Vaswani always gave us the example of the sun. The sun always gives; it gives its light and warmth and energy to all the universe. The earth gives its natural treasures to others. The tree gives its fruits for others and does not retain any for itself. The river also flows to quench the thirst of others and not for itself. Learn this important lesson that Mother Nature teaches us. "To give" is one of the fundamental laws of nature.

2. We should not consider ourselves to be 'owners' of anything. None of our possessions are our own. Everything is created by Him.

All the things, tangible or intangible belong to God. This realisation will bring detachment. By giving up the ownership of all that you aspire to

God, you become free of every bondage.

The world is a stage and in this drama of life we are merely actors; each of us is here to play a part. We move and act according to the directions from above. This attitude brings a sense of detachment. For, we know everything is part of a Divine drama and that the whole drama will eventually come to an end.

A man with this realisation lives for God. All his actions are without any expectation or reward. Such a man is detached from the world and nearer to God.

We become totally free when we surrender ourselves completely to the Lord. Complete surrender gives us freedom from fear and worry, because complete surrender is the path of bliss.

3. **We should consider ourselves as travellers or pilgrims upon this earth. This planet is not our native home. It is a 'Travellers' Inn' and our stay here is short. It is possible that at the Travellers' Inn, we may meet people, or make good friends, but after a short stay we must all go our separate ways to our own destinations.**

Ko Kahu Ko Nahi, Preetam Jan le Mann Mahi.
"No one is mine, except the Lord."

We should do our duty and maybe a little more. But we should do it with a sense of detachment. This is the teaching of the great ones. Gurudev Sadhu Vaswani has said, "This planet earth is a vast desert. In this desert we live as travellers."

4. **The last and most important way is the Socratic injunction: 'Know Thyself'.**

Once we realise the truth of our being, we would be able to overcome our attachments. For, all attachments are either physical, emotional or mental. But man is neither the physical body nor the mind; the truth is, man enshrines the *Atman*. And *Atman* is *shakti*. Once man realises this that all that he wants and all that he needs is within him, he will not have to wander outside. He will not run after money, fame, and name. Such a man is not 'bound' to the world, but is a free bird in the firmament of the spirit.

What is your reaction to the above? Difficult to practise? Remember, this is not an exercise for a day or two. It must become your attitude to life, for your lifetime!

Chapter - VI

Dhyana Yoga

This chapter gives us the Lord's teachings on *Dhyana Yoga* or the *Yoga* of Meditation. True renunciation is not formal *sannyasa,* but the renunciation of the desire for the fruits of action. We are told about the Path of Meditation and the Power of Prayer. This teaches us the *yoga* of equanimity, the *yoga* that enables us to perceive the One in All and the All in One.

What happens in this chapter

Thus far, we have learnt about the value of *Karma Yoga* by which we renounce not actions themselves, but the fruits of action. This kind of desireless action, we have been told, brings about purity of mind. In this Chapter we are taught to appreciate the value of a purified mind, and how we may attain to God by meditating effectively on Him with a pure mind. For when we renounce selfish purpose, when we walk the way of disinterested action, we allow the Divine Will to work through us.

> For the sage who wishes to attain to *yoga*, action is said to be the means: for the same sage, when he has attained to *yoga*, serenity is said to be the means.
> [VI:3]

How may we attain to this state of serenity? Sri Krishna actually explains to Arjuna, a little of the technique of meditation.

1. Choose a pure, quiet place.

2. Choose a steady and not too high seat.

3. Restrain the mind and senses, the mind must be free from lower desires if you wish to meditate and go into inward stillness.

4. Sit motionless, with body, head and neck held erect with a fixed gaze focussed on the tip of the nose.

5. With a heart, serene and fearless, hold your mind from its restless roaming, and lose your thoughts, and your self in the immensity of the Lord's Being.

The object of *Dhyana Yoga* is to meditate on Him, the Lord, the Beloved of the Soul, and so to attain union with Him.

He who would attain to meditation must walk the middle path. He must be temperate in all his activities; he must adopt the golden mean between the extremes of asceticism and indulgence. Such a man lives in the world, but is detached from the world. His focus, his goal, his joy is in God-realisation. He renounces desires; he restrains his senses; he eliminates fear, and rests his mind in the *Atman.* He develops *samadrishti,* that the One *Atman* which resides within him, resides also in all things, all creatures, all forms of life. He realises that he can never purchase happiness for himself with the suffering of others.

Arjuna observes that the fickle, turbulent, strong and obstinate mind is very difficult to control. How then, can we attain to the *yoga* of equanimity?

The Lord offers two ways:

1. *Abhyasa* or constant practice

2. *Vairagy*a or dispassion, absence of desire

> *Yoga* is hard to attain by one who is not self-controlled. But by the self-controlled it is attainable by striving through proper means. Such is My conviction.[VI:36]

What of the man who strives, but does not succeed?

The Lord assures us that no man who is a sincere seeker can come to an evil end. Our striving, our efforts at self-realisation will eventually help us. We need never despair, for the Lord is all love and compassion, and will not let our sincere efforts go in vain. We will rise, step by step, to realisation.

Thus the Gita holds out to every seeker the hope, nay, the promise, that though he falls a hundred times, he will rise again! His failures are only temporary.

The *tapasvi* (ascetic) inflicts severe penances on his body; the *gnani* (knower of the Vedas) is learned and wise; the *karmi* (man of activity) is hard working and sincere. But greater than them all is the true *yogi.* And the best of *yogis,* according to the Gita, is he who offers to the Lord his love and devotion, and worships Him in faith.

> And, of all yogis, he who, full of faith adoreth Me, with his Self abiding in Me, he is deemed by Me to be the most completely harmonised (the most devoted).
>
> [VI:47]

Think About it...

Having explained *Karma Yoga* in all its essential aspects, the Lord now turns to the Path of Meditation or Communion through Meditation. One vital fact that this chapter emphasises is that *Karma Yoga, Gnana Yoga* and *Dhyana Yoga* are not ends in themselves; they are all paths to attain the one goal: and this goal is not just self-realisation or *atma sakshatkara.* That too, is only a means to a greater goal, the ultimate goal of life – that is, God-realisation.

For Your Reflection

Have you heard of this beautiful incident in the Mahabharata, where Guru Dronacharya is teaching his royal pupils to concentrate their attention on the chosen target? He points to a parrot, perched on the green and leafy branch of a tree, completely camouflaged in the greenery all around. One by one, the Kaurava and Pandava princes are asked to come under the tree and take aim at the parrot: only to take aim, not to shoot their arrows.

Each prince comes as the Guru calls out his name. Each strings his bow, fixes his arrow, and takes aim.

"What do you see?" asks the Guru of each one, as he stands beneath the tree and looks up at the bird.

"I can see the green leaves fluttering in the wind," one replies.

"The glare of the sunlight through the leaves almost blinds me," says another.

And so they come and go; one can hardly see the parrot for the leaves; another sees glimpses of the blue sky above; one complains that the bird is barely visible.

"I can see its sharp, brown claws and its pointed, red beak clearly!" exclaims Duryodhana. "I see the bird clearly!"

The last to take aim is Arjuna, the guru's favourite disciple. He too comes and takes aim, looking up steadily, directly.

"What do you see?" the Guru asks again.

"I see only the eye of the parrot," Arjuna replies.

"What else do you see?" the Guru asks. "Can you see the leaves, the sunlight trickling through the leaves, from the blue sky beyond?"

"I can see none of these," replies Arjuna. "I can only see the eye of the parrot."

This is concentration — The ability to focus vision, thought and mind in a unified function. Concentration is the starting point as well as the basic aim of all meditation. We cannot meditate until we learn to concentrate; and the more we meditate, the more we grow in the power of concentration.

The Chinese sage Chuang–Tzu relates an interesting story. There was a man who used to forge swords for the Minister of War. He was eighty years old, and yet his work was perfect. He never once slipped.

The Minister of War once asked him, "What is it that makes your work perfect? Just your inborn ability, the skill you have acquired or is it the method you follow?"

"It is none of these," the old man replied. "It is just concentration. I started forging swords when I was twenty years old. I cared for nothing else. If a thing were not a sword, I simply did not notice it. I just gave all my energy and effort and attention to making swords."

Concentration has been defined by a wise teacher as wholeness, unity and equilibrium, a unification of the senses and the faculties. They must work in unified harmony.

Meditation is not possible without concentration. And I don't just mean lower levels of concentration such as we use at work or in the laboratory. I mean the kind of higher concentration in which the mind gathers its full strength through singleness, becoming steadfast and focussed, attaining union with the One. This is what Socrates refers to when he says: Thought is best when the mind is gathered into herself and is aspiring after true being.

The practice of unified, single-minded focus on one subject, is concentration. When it is turned inward, it becomes meditation. As Sri Krishna tells us in the Bhagavad Gita:

As a lamp placed in a windless spot does not flicker, nor does a yogi of subdued mind practising union with the self.

Questions:

1. Are you one of those people who find it difficult to practise meditation?

2. Do you find it difficult to control your thoughts?

3. Do you lack time to sit and meditate?

   The following section is specially for people like you.

Think about it...

The great Maharishi Patanjali himself warns us about the *antarayas* or obstacles which we encounter on the path of *yoga* and these also apply to meditation, the journey within:

1. Illness: when you are in a disturbed frame of mind or physically unfit, you cannot meditate successfully. Patanjali warns us that meditation should not be taught to those who lack emotional balance and maturity. Negative states of mind like arrogance, anger, hostility and hatred are also not conducive to meditation. We must also realise that physical ailments affect both body and mind. It is better that we do not begin to practise meditation in such conditions.

2. Lethargy or *tamas* is a state induced by overeating, overindulgence, or occasionally even by extreme weather conditions. We feel low and depleted; we feel 'heavy' in body and mind; we find that we cannot do anything useful or constructive. Our moods have a definite bearing on our minds, and it is better that we avoid such conditions.

3. Doubt or *samasya* is a negative feeling which fills us with uncertainty and pessimism. This can also undermine our effort to meditate.

4. Haste, leading to rashness and impatience is not suited for the practise of meditation. We will only slip instead of making progress on the path.

5. Fatigue or exhaustion, known as *alasya* is also a debilitating condition. Our confidence is undermined, our energy levels are low. We need to be rejuvenated, remotivated before we can embark on meditation.

6. Distraction or *avirati* disturbs our powers of concentration. It diverts our mind from the chosen path and may even lead us to needless temptations. When we are led in

the wrong direction, we lose the power of concentration.

7. Arrogance and pride are serious hurdles on the path of meditation. Those who are satisfied, complacent and vain, think that they know everything; they are in a state of *avidya* or ignorance and they cannot focus on meditation.

8. There is also the sense of an inability to proceed. We are discouraged and disheartened by what we perceive as our failure to progress. We may have even taken the first few steps, but feel that we are not getting anywhere. We despair of ever achieving our goal. This is hardly a helpful attitude.

9. Loss of Confidence is the consequence of our own inability to proceed. We fall back and lose the motivation to pursue our goal.

These obstacles, as I have said, are mentioned by Patanjali. But they are not all. Living in a modern world of allurements and entanglements, we face many more such obstacles or "attitude problems".

1. "I have no time!" we proclaim loudly. We have time for TV, time to gossip, time to fool around,

time to 'browse the web' mindlessly, but no time for ourselves, no time to discover the hidden treasures within us.

2. "I don't live alone!" we protest. Friends, family, colleagues, neighbours, customers and business contacts are all entitled to their claims upon us. We respect their demands, but we ignore our own deeper needs.

3. "I have other needs!" we insist. We are anxious to make more money; we are eager to become more powerful; we seek fame and popularity, and we decide that meditation and the inner world can wait.

Students of *yoga,* aspirants who wish to learn meditation, wherever they may be, have this in common: they value inner peace, harmony and serenity. They are eager and determined to probe the depths of the true Self, and they have made a serious commitment to the way of *abhyasa.* And in order to succeed on the chosen path, they make every effort to conquer both outer distractions and inner impediments.

In the Gita, we are given a memorable picture of a tortoise. Once the tortoise draws in its limbs, you will not be able to draw them out, even if you cut the creature into four pieces! This is the kind of determination you too, will need, if you wish to tread the way of *abhyasa*.

How may we achieve this?

1. We must pray, again and again.

2. We must seek the guidance of a Guru, a spiritual mentor.

3. We must start with *Karma Yoga*, before we set out in search of the inner self.

4. We must cultivate self-discipline.

5. We must learn to eat right. *Sattvic* food, food of non-violence will provide us with the right energy and the right frame of mind to pursue the path of *abhyasa*.

6. We must offer all that we are, all that we have, all that we do, to the Lord, in a spirit of *arpanam*.

Chapter - VII

Gnana Vignana Yoga

What is the difference between *gnana* and *vignana*?

To know the essence *(tattva)* of *nirguna nirakara paramatman* (attributeless, formless Supreme Reality) is *gnana*; to know the *leela* of *saguna sakara* (God in incarnate human form with all His Divine attributes) is *vignana*. The former is *Brahman*; the latter is *Bhagwan*.

In this chapter, we get to hear of *Brahman* and *Bhagwan*. Sri Krishna is manifested God. Knowledge becomes realisation when we see the Eternal on the plane of manifestation. We also get to know about the four types of people who worship Him.

Lokamanya Tilak, in his Gita *Rahasya*, defines *gnana* as spiritual knowledge and *vignana* as specified knowledge.

What happens in this chapter

The Lord gives us an explanation of His Manifested state. In short, it is thus: all that exists, is nothing but the manifestation of the Lord Himself. He is the cause of the appearance of the Universe – and all things in it. The earth, water, fire, air, ether, mind, intellect and ego, the lower *prakriti*, make up His eightfold nature. His is also the life-element which upholds and sustains the Universe and makes it active.

> There is naught whatsoever higher than I, O Arjuna! All that is here is threaded on Me as rows of pearls are threaded on a single string. [VII:7]

He is in all creation, yet beyond all creation. He is the fresh taste in the waters; He is the light in the moon and sun; He is the *Shabda* in all the *Vedas;* He is the fragrance of the earth; He is the life in all that lives; He is the wisdom of the wise, and the splendour in all that is splendid. He is the One in all.

Alas, the world, deluded by the three *gunas*, fails to see His Divine Manifestation in all that is!

We are also told of four types of *bhaktas* who worship the Lord for different reasons – to seek success in their undertakings (the *artharthi bhaktas*); to seek protection in distress (the *arthah bhaktas*); to seek illumination (*jignasu bhaktas);* and lastly, those who seek Him, and Him alone. These are the *gnani bhaktas,* who are truly beloved of the Lord. To them, the world is a vision of God. The Lord makes this promise to them:

> Those who know Me as the One that underlies the elements (*adhibuta*), and the Gods (*adhidaiva*), and all sacrifice (*adhiyagna*), they, harmonised in mind, know Me even in the hour of death.   [VII:30]

Sri Krishna knows the value of the other three types of devotees. It is no sin to seek God's grace for worldly success, alleviation of suffering and acquisition of knowledge. Many of them are capable of deep devotion. But enveloped by *yoga maya* (illusion that goes with creation) they fail to see the One in all. Truly beloved of the Lord are the *gnani bhaktas:* "For they come unto Me!" avers Sri Krishna.

Think About it...

Most of us are driven by our inherent nature and ignorance to seek the powers of minor deities, or to seek the Lord's grace for worldly gifts. In

His compassion, the Lord concedes: "Whichever devotee seeks to worship with faith whatever form, I make that very faith steadfast."

As the ancient scriptures tell us:

Aakaashaat Patitam Toyam Yathaa Gachchhati Saagaram

Sarvadevanamaskaara Keshavam Prati Gachchhati ||

As all the water falling from the sky ultimately ends up in the ocean, the prayers/tributes offered to all the gods ultimately reach the One God, Keshava.

For Your Reflection

There was a King who received great comfort and solace from the wise words of a holy man. Grateful beyond words, he wanted to express his appreciation, and offered him an expensive gift, of a pair of golden slippers.

The holy man smiled. He wanted to make the King understand that worldly gifts were unsuitable to someone who had chosen the life of the Spirit.

"O King," he said, "If I accept this gift, you must also give me fine clothes to match these golden slippers."

"And so I will," promised the King readily. "You will have royal robes studded with gems and precious stones."

"But your Highness," said the holy man, "would it not appear ridiculous if I wore royal robes and golden slippers and move on my own feet from place to place?"

"That's easily settled," said the King. "I will give you the best Arabian mare from my stable, for you to ride on."

"Hmm," said the holy man thoughtfully. "Would it not be strange for a man to have all this, and lack a beautiful abode, a lovely wife and servants?"

"All this, I shall arrange for you to have," the King assured him.

"But then sire," said the holy man, "If I should have a son, and if he should chance to die, will you bear my grief and weep instead of me?"

"How could I do that for you?" said the King, startled out of his fit of generosity. "You must bear your own grief, you must weep for yourself."

"Then, O King," said the holy man, "I will not take the golden slippers, the golden robes, the Arabian mare, the beautiful house and servants, or the lovely wife! I do not wish to be led into pain and misery."

The King understood the message. He realised that material things, identification with the physical, can never lead to true joy. The holy man, who was a true gnani bhakta, had actually initiated him on the path of true realisation.

What we need, more than material wealth, is gnana, the wealth of the spirit, for it offers us the freedom of liberation from maya!

Questions:

Here are a few questions that people often ask me: Is it wrong to aspire for wealth? Is material

112

wealth and worldly happiness an impediment on the path of spirituality? Is it wrong to call upon God for help when we are in distress? Who else can we turn to, if not to our Divine Father?

I am also going to give you my own answer to the above questions: when you begin to tread the path of spiritual awareness, then you will find that you do not really aspire to material possessions, worldly goals and desires. You leave it to the Lord.

It is for God to give you whatever He likes. God is our Master, and let me assure you, He is a very benevolent Master! Spiritual awareness helps you to surrender the thread of your life in His safe, benevolent hands, and you will find miracles happening in your daily life.

Yearn for the Lord even as a miser yearns for gold. Yearn for the Lord even as a child who has lost its mother yearns for her presence. Yearn for the Lord even as a lover yearns for his beloved!
— Sri Ramakrishna Paramahansa

Practical Suggestions

Here are a few practical suggestions that will enable you to cultivate the spirit of the *gnani bhakta,* even while you go about your worldly duties:

* Be still! From time to time, as often as I can, in the midst of daily work, of tumult and tempest, I pause for a brief moment and lift up my heart in loving converse with God. I speak to Him as I speak to my dear mother or to a loving friend. My words are not carefully prepared, nor are they necessarily quotations from the scriptures. What I speak to God flows naturally and spontaneously out of the purity and simplicity of my heart.

  One day, as Gurudev Sadhu Vaswani lay on his bed of sickness, these were the words on his lips:

  My heart, O Lord, is thirsty for Thy Light and Thy Love!
  Come to me each day, in my thoughts and aspirations.

  Come to me in my dreams, in the laughter on my lips, in the tears in my eyes.

  In my worship and my work, in life and in death, come Thou to me.

  Be Thou with me in Thy Mercy and Thy Love!

Bring the heart back to the sweet, familiar presence of God. Be still and let the peace of God flow into you! It is only when the soul is at peace that true work is done, and the body and mind have the strength to bear and endure.

* *Be Calm!* Let me do nothing that may disturb my peace of mind and heart. Let my daily life be so regulated as to strengthen the inner calm, not take away from it. So let me avoid overwork. And let me not be in a hurry to do anything. Let me go about my work quietly, gently and lovingly, my mind and heart devoted to the Lotus Feet of the Lord. Then will my soul become strong and all around me the world will smile.

* Seek God! In the midst of my work – aye, even in the midst of my *kirtan* and worship – let me, again and again, withdraw for a brief while into the inner chamber of my heart and there speak to God, gaze upon His Beauteous Face. Let me do this from time to time throughout the day and night. Truly blessed are these brief moments of intimate contact with God, when I penetrate into the very depths of my soul and offer all I have and all I am to Him and feel grateful to Him for His everlasting mercy and loving tenderness.

This may not be accomplished within a day, a week, or a month. But nothing is impossible to him who, in faith and devotion, treads the Way of abhyasa, the Path of Practice. Does not the Lord declare in the Gita —

However difficult or impossible it may seem,
You, O Arjuna, may still achieve it
By steadfast effort and wholehearted devotion
So walk the way of practice!

And as the Chinese say: "The journey of a thousand miles begins with one step." We may be far, very far, from the goal. But even if we have taken a single step in the right direction, we have advanced on the spiritual path. And for every single step that we take to reach God, God takes a hundred steps to draw nearer to us. For while we think we are seeking God, in reality it is God who is in search of us!

Chapter - VIII

Akshara Brahman Yoga

This has been translated as "The Yoga of the Imperishable *Brahman*". In his own inimitable way, Gurudev Sadhu Vaswani called it "The Path of Light".

The Path of Light is that which will lead us to God — to the Supreme Eternal State of Peace and Blessedness. He is *Akshara Brahman* — the Supreme Indestructible and Imperishable Reality.

What happens in this chapter

Arjuna has crucial questions that the Lord answers first. What are the following, he requests the Lord to tell him: *1) Brahma; 2) Adhyatman; 3) Karma; 4) Adhiyagna; 5) Adhibhuta; 6) Adhidhaiva.*

These terms are explained by the Lord.

Arjuna also begs the Lord to enlighten him on that *yoga* which one may practise even in *antakala,* the hour of death, and so attain to the Supreme. The Lord's reply is succinct:

> He, who, casting off the body, goeth forth, meditating upon Me alone, at the hour of death, he attaineth to My State (*madbhavam*). Doubt that not! [VIII:5]

Think of the Lord and do your duty! When these two are linked together, we are sure to reach the Lord.

> Arjuna, he who constantly thinketh upon Me with a mind that regardeth none else, he, the *yogi*, *nitya–yuktah* (ever harmonised, always absorbed in Me), he easily attaineth Me. [VIII:14]

This then is the secret of *yoga,* to remember God constantly.

The Universe has come into being, and dissolved through several *yugas*. Several such time-cycles have come and gone. There is no end to the process of birth, death and re-birth, until we attain to the Eternal. He, the Highest, may be reached by unswerving devotion.

> Having known all this, the *yogi* passes beyond all merit that comes from the study of the Vedas, from sacrifices *(yagna),* from austerities *(tapas)* and holy gifts (*dana*), and goeth to the Supreme Eternal State (of Peace and Blessedness).   [VIII:28]

Think About it...

This is the law: what a man looks for at the hour of his death, to that he goes. The soul is fashioned to its like. The thought of a man's last moment determines his destiny after his death. A man is transformed to that state *(bhava)* which he bears in mind when casting off his body. He, whose soul, at the hour of death, is fixed in meditation on Krishna, on abandoning the body (the "shell"), comes to Krishna after death. But there are other destinations for those who, while quitting the body, think not of Krishna but of other beings, other objects. As a man thinketh in the hour of death, so he becometh after death.

Does he think of earthly objects, of father, mother, brother, friend, wife, child, wealth, power, honour, gain? Then he cometh back to this earth.

Does he think of Heaven and Heavenly happiness? Then he goeth to Heaven, the *swarga loka,* which is an abode of bliss, but a temporary one.

Does he think only of the Supreme? Then to the Supreme he goeth after death. This is Ultimate Liberation - *Moksha.*

This, then, is the law: whatever be the *bhava,* state, object, being, a God, man, beast, bird, worm, tree, place, land, money, etc., whereof a man constantly thinks, doing his *abhyasa* in daily life, that *bhava* dominates his consciousness in the hour of his departure. And in that *bhava* is fashioned the picture of his life after death.

Questions:

We know that all that is born must die. Death is the one unalterable verity of human life.

But, how many of us understand the meaning of death?

What is Death?

What kind of an experience brings down the curtain on the drama of our life?

If truth must be told, many of us are so superstitious about discussing death; we are frightened by the very word death. We shy away from the very word, the very thought of death.

What makes us so afraid to die?

Where do you think we will go after death?

Where would you like to go after death?

Death and After...

According to Vedanta wisdom, there are four possibilities open to the soul after death:

1. For one who has attained enlightenment during this life, there is total liberation from the cycle of birth and death. Such a one attains *sadyah mukti* or instantaneous liberation and is not born again.

2. For one who has not attained liberation, but achieved purity of mind and devotion to *Brahman,* there is a force which pushes the soul beyond the pull of this world and towards liberation. This is *Karma Mukti,* which gives us gradual or sequential liberation. In this process, the soul is led along a path of light and so attains an increasing expansion in consciousness until liberation is attained.

3. For one who has tried to live a virtuous life, but is not ready for liberation, there is a finite period of existence on the astral plane, where the astral body experiences pleasurable conditions. This is known as *Swarga.* It is not liberation, but a relative experience of pleasure. This finite period is brought to an end when the soul's good *karma* is exhausted, and the soul is re-born into a new life.

4. For one who has accumulated no good *karma* at all, there is the painful fourth alternative, a period of intense suffering. But this period also comes to a close when the sinful *karma* is exhausted, and the soul is re-born in a new embodiment.

Thus, in the first two cases, liberation is attained. In the third and the fourth, the soul must return to earth for the sake of its further evolution, after a period of either heavenly pleasure or hellish suffering. In these cases, *karma* will determine its next embodiment. For there are residues, remnants of *karma* that are not exhausted in the life-after-death state, be it heaven or hell. It is this residue or remnant that influences one's rebirth and life experiences. In other words, none of us is born into this world with what is called a clean slate. Even what we consider to be hereditary traits are in reality determined by the *karma* of previous lives.

Rabbi Eleazer said, "Repent one day before your death."

Said his pupils, "Does man know when he would die?" He answered, "Then he surely must repent today, lest he die tomorrow."   *Anonymous*

Chapter - IX

Rajavidya Rajaguhya Yoga

Gurudev Sadhu Vaswani translated this title as "The Supreme Mystery".

The great German poet Goethe referred to the "eternal secret that floats around us". In this Chapter, Sri Krishna speaks to His dear disciple Arjuna of the "Eternal Secret". "I shall tell thee the most secret truth," He tells Arjuna.

This is the truth regarding His Transcendent Being. It is the Divine Mystery of the Lord. It is *gnana* with *vignana* combined. It is awareness of His Supreme Being and the knowledge of His Divine love for us. This is both the Soveriegn Science and the Sovereign Secret.

The sacred Truth of the Lord's Divine Mystery is now unfolded to us – God pervades all the Universe; all things are rooted in Him, but He is not rooted in them. He transcends the Universe. He is the Eternal, universal *Atman* that pervades creation. By fixing our minds on Him, by worshipping Him, we can reach Him.

What happens in this chapter

Arjuna's devotion, his earnest questioning and his genuine aspiration to learn the truth have all proved that he is the true disciple. And therefore, the Lord now declares to him the great secret — or the 'secret truth':

> By Me the whole Universe is pervaded in My unmanifest aspect. All beings have root in Me, but I am not rooted in them. And (yet) the things have no root in Me. Behold My Divine Mystery, My Self Creates all, Sustaineth all, yet is not rooted in them. [IX:4-5]

Alas, those of us who are ignorant, do not recognise the Lord's Supreme nature. Evolved, enlightened souls, on the other hand, realise that He is the One behind the all, and worship Him with a fixed mind and unceasing devotion. Such men, who have sought their ultimate refuge in the Lord, are taken care of in every respect.

What is the kind of devotion that pleases the Lord? In one of the most beautiful and most quoted verses of the Gita, the Lord tells us:

> Whatever thou doest, whatever thou eatest, whatever thou offerest, whatever thou givest away, whatever austerities thou dost practise, let it all be done, O Arjuna, as an offering unto Me. [IX:27]

When all our actions, thoughts and words are offered to God as Krishna *Arpanam,* we are freed from the bonds of *karma.* Therefore, the way is clear:

> Fix thy mind on Me; be devoted to Me; worship Me; bow down to Me. Thus having controlled thyself, and making Me thy goal supreme, thou shalt come unto Me.　　　　　　　　　　　　　　　　　　[IX:34]

Think About it...

The Lord makes another promise to us in this chapter, in one of the most well known and beloved *slokas* of the Gita:

> Those who worship Me and meditate on Me alone, to them who are self-controlled, I give what they have not and hold secure whatever they have.　　[IX-22]

To those who worship Him, meditate on Him and place their trust in Him, Sri Krishna offers all security. He guards their welfare. He gives them the full assurance of blessedness. He gives them eternal Happiness.

What more can we ask of the Lord?

For Your Reflection

Sri Ramana Maharishi once narrated the following story to illustrate this sloka.

There was a sincere devotee of the Lord, who was bound by his karma to live in dire poverty. Very often, his family had nothing to eat, and his wife always blamed him for their enforced starvation.

Once it so happened that the entire family had to go without food for four consecutive days. Unable to bear the constant complaints and taunts of his wife, he took his palm-leaf manuscript of the Bhagavad Gita; with a piece of charcoal he cut out the words 'Yogakshemam Vahamyaham' *(I attend to all his needs and welfare)* from the Ninth Chapter.

In this mood of frustration and bitterness, he went to the river to take his morning bath. While he was out, a cart full of provisions arrived at his house, brought by a young and radiant boy. There were enough provisions loaded on the cart to last the family for a month. The handsome boy started unloading the provisions, when the devotee's wife stopped him. "There must be some mistake," she insisted. "Who sent these provisions with you? Are you sure they are meant for this house?"

"Of course they are meant for your family!" the

boy assured her. "Your husband, who is my master, arranged for these to be bought and delivered here as soon as possible."

The wife was speechless with amazement. "My husband is your master?" she asked him in amazement. "Yes indeed," the boy replied, busily arranging the provisions inside her tiny kitchen. Just then the wife noticed that there was a deep and angry red gash on the boy's forehead, from which fresh blood was still oozing out. Concerned, she asked the young lad how he had hurt himself so badly.

"I was a little late carrying out my task," the lad explained sheepishly. "My master lost his temper with me this morning."

Soon thereafter the devotee returned from the river, and was amazed to see his wife and children in a happy and cheerful mood. They thanked him profusely for the arrangements he had made, and informed him that a hot meal was ready, and they were only waiting for his arrival so that he could offer the food to the Lord as naivedya, before they all sat down and ate together.

The devotee was flabbergasted. But before he could even ask anything further, the wife chided him gently: "How could you be so rude and cruel to that handsome lad, your servant? I was quite shocked to see how badly you had hit him!"

"My servant? But I have no servant..." stammered the man. He was even more amazed when he was shown all the provisions and told about the handsome young boy who had delivered them that morning.

He was overwhelmed with grief and shame when he understood that it was Lord Krishna Himself who had personally come as a boy to prove the truth of His promise to us in the Gita. He realised that the gash on the boy's forehead had been inflicted when he angrily cut out the words in the Gita.

Thousands upon thousands of people must have had such incidents happening to them in their own life! The Lord's love for us works in the most amazing and mysterious ways, and comes to our rescue when we are in dire straits.

Questions:

Are you worried about your future?

Do you often feel afraid about your savings and the future provisions made for your family?

What causes maximum stress to you, the loss of your regular income/loss of job? Old age? Fear of illness/accidents? Or the future of your children?

Does the discharge of your duties towards your family leave you tense and anxious?

Practical Suggestions:

You too, can learn to place your trust in the Lord, and let go of your cares and anxieties. Here are a few practical suggestions to help you hand over the reins of your life into His capable hands:

1. Firstly cultivate the habit of accepting every situation, every circumstance as the 'Will of God'. Acceptance with due gratitude is also a subtle law, which puts you on the path of self-growth. "O God, whatever You do and whatever happens has a purpose and a meaning. Your scheme of things is perfect. I accept Your Will." This should be your attitude in life; and whether you succeed or fail, ever remain grateful to God!

   Gurudev Sadhu Vaswani in his sacred verses has said,

   Thank You, Thank You, O Lord,

   Grateful to You,

   Wherever I am.

   Whatever I am.

   Shukur. I accept it all.

2. Secondly, whenever there are hurdles in life or problems beyond your control, seek God's help. To cross the hurdles, to solve the problems and to meet the challenges of life, you need inner strength. You can get this strength by appealing to the Supreme *Shakti,* the All-Powerful, the Almighty. Seek His strength. Appeal to Him: O Supreme *Shakti,* give me strength.

3. Thirdly, you have to train the mind. The mind, as our scriptures tell us, often behaves like a drunken monkey or like a wild horse. It has to be controlled; it is to be trained to shun negativism. Negative thoughts are a habit of the mind. Dispel negative thoughts and invite positive thoughts instead. You will find a change for the better in your life. Be firm with your mind. Resolve, here and now, that you will put up a 'No Entry' board to negativism. Block the rush of negative thoughts. Resolve, too, that you will put up the 'Welcome' sign and greet all positive thoughts. Convert your negative thoughts into positive ones. Replace the negative with the positive. You will experience calm and soothing vibrations not only within but also in your surroundings.

4. Fourthly, believe that 'This too shall pass away'. Tell yourself. "This trying time is here to test my faith. This stressful period will get over soon." For at the end of every tunnel is light, at the end of a dark night there is the beautiful dawn. The clouds spreading darkness hide the bright shining sun. Once the clouds pass away, the sun will be visible, shining ever bright, spreading its warm radiance and light!

5. Fifthly, keep your mind fully occupied. This will not only keep you away from worry and other wasteful thoughts, but will make the mind strong and constructive. Above all, learn to use your energy in the service of others. Pray for people who face greater difficulties than you do, for God knows that there are many of them. This will uplift your mind. Be an instrument of God and plough His field. Engage your mind in *satsang*. Read inspirational literature. As it is said:

Lives of great men all remind us

We can make our lives sublime…

6. Sixthly, you should always remember, that God is with you. Tell yourself constantly: He

is my Father and Mother. He is the One who protects all of us at all times. We have to have a direct hotline with God! You should talk to Him; have a dialogue with Him and sure enough He will show you the way. Build up faith in Him. Believe in Him.

If all else fails you, remember the Lord's promise to us in the Gita: "Renouncing all rites and writ duties, come to Me for single refuge" – seek refuge at His Holy Feet. He will never ever let you down!

Chapter - X

Vibhuti Yoga

Vibhuti Yoga is translated as "the Yoga of Divine Manifestation". Sri Krishna continues with the revelation of His Divine Self in this chapter. His immanent, transcendent Self is manifested in all that is; He is the Source of all, and in knowing Him, we know the All-in-all.

What happens in this chapter

In this chapter, Sri Krishna recounts, or rather reiterates to Arjuna, His divine attributes: 1) His Lordship or Power over all created beings; 2) His immanence in them. He is the immanent energy, the indwelling Essence, the Source of all. The true *yogis,* knowing this, are absorbed in Krishna, and therefore filled with the joy of His presence. But we do not have to go looking for Him; for in His Divine compassion, Sri Krishna is also the indweller in the heart of the true *bhakta.*

> Hear again, O Arjuna, My Supreme word. From a desire to do thee good, I will declare it to thee, for thou art My Beloved. [X:1]

Whatever we see around us, is an aspect of the Lord, a reflection of His glory and power and Supreme Energy:

> I am the source of all spiritual and material worlds. Everything emanates from Me. The wise who perfectly know this engage in My devotional service and worship Me with all their hearts. [X:8]

Whatever we behold around us, the grand, the magnificent, the pleasant, the beautiful and the mighty, Krishna is in them all. He is the wisdom of the wise ones; He is the beauty, courage, wonder, purity and power in all that is most beautiful, most courageous, and the most wonderful, pure and powerful.

I am Prahlada among the demons, I am time among those who keep calculations, I am King (Lion) among the beasts and I am the son of Vinata (Garud) among the birds.

I am Wind among the purifying agents, I am Rama among those wielding weapons (warriors), of Fishes I am Alligator, and amongst the Rivers I am Ganga (Ganges).

I am the beginning, the end and the middle of the creations, O Arjuna, of the sciences I am the science of the self *(brahma-vidya)*, of those who argue and debate I am the argument.

Of the letters I am *Alpha* (the beginning 'Akaar'), of the compound verbs I am the dual, I am also the imperishable time and I am the creator and upholder whose face is turned to all the sides.

I am all consuming and all devouring death, I am the cause (seed) of all that has to come to be and of feminine being, I am fame, prosperity, speech, memory, intelligence, steadfastness and patience.

And likewise, I am *Brihatsama* among the hymns, of the *Mantras* I am *Gayatri*, I am *Margashrisha* among the months, and I am Spring among the seasons.

[X: 30-35]

His glory is infinite. He is the Self enshrined in the heart of every creature. From Him all beings arise; by Him they live; and at His word they all depart and meet their end. Whatever is good and true and powerful, is but a fragment of His splendour. And yet not all these glorious manifestations can wholly reflect or exhaust Him or even capture a fraction of His glory.

All the best qualities – wisdom, forgiveness, non-delusion, truth, *ahimsa*, equanimity, contentment, austerity and charity, arise from the Lord. He is the root and essence of everything. The word used by the Lord is *vibhuti* – meaning glory or sovereignity; and also suggesting an idea of all-pervasion and immanence. In other words, the whole Universe, in all its splendour and magnificence, is but a fragment of the Lord's Divine Self.

But of what use to thee, O Arjuna, is this detailed knowledge? I sustain this whole Universe, pervading it with but one fragment of Myself: and I abide! [X:42]

Think About it...

Sri Krishna has touched upon *Bhakti Yoga* in the ninth chapter: in this tenth chapter, he inspires, inculcates and sustains *Bhakti* in Arjuna, as in all his devotees, by dwelling on what Sri Ramanujacharya calls His *anantha kalyana guna* (multitudes of auspicious attributes) and His sovereignty over the universe, which is uncontested, unrivalled and matchless. The Universe is ruled by His Will and He is its Origin and Support. He who knows this, is the Lord's true devotee; he who knows this, lives in the joy of the Lord's presence; he who knows this, knows the Lord!

For Your Reflection

The man whispered: "God, speak to me",

and the meadow lark sang.

But the man did not hear!

So the man yelled: **God, speak to me.**

And God rolled the thunder across the sky.

But the man did not listen!

He looked around and said, "God, let me see you."
And a star shone brightly.

But the man did not see!

And, he shouted, "God, show me a miracle."

And a life was born!

But the man did not notice!

So, he cried out in despair,

"God, touch me."

Whereupon, God reached down and gently touched
the man.

But the man brushed the butterfly away ....

and walked on, disappointed.

He could not see God anywhere, because he failed
to see Him everywhere and in all beings.

A realised person experiences God in many ways:

in the chirping of the birds,

in the roll of the thunder,

in the twinkling light of the stars,

in the miracle of the birth of a child,

and in the soft touch of a butterfly.

He sees God everywhere and experiences God in everything.

He sings in tune with the *Mantra:*

Isaavasyam Idam Sarvam

All that is, is a vesture of the Lord.

Questions:

1. Have you ever asked yourself who created this magnificent universe and the beautiful world you live in?

2. He who created space and time, don't you think He must be beyond space and time?

3. How far away do you think He is from you? How long do you think it will be before you can reach Him?

4. If, as this chapter of the Gita reveals to us, God envelopes all things and He is indwelling everything, how would you live in this world? What kind of vision will condition your

perceptions? What would be your attitude to the other creatures that breathe the breath of life?

Practical Suggestions:

If you want to live a life of beauty and joy, then you must make prayer an integral part of your life. If you wish to make your prayers truly effective, you must realise that God is with you, always.

How can you make God real in your life? How can you practise the presence of God in your life?

1. Pray to God, meditate on His creation, meditate on nature, walk around a beautiful park or up a hillock, travel to a scenic spot or a hill station, admire God's beautiful creation, examine a flower, a petal, a stem, a blade of grass. And marvel at the beauty and perfection of Nature. Every flower, every petal, every stem, is perfection and holds the secrets of nature.

2. Choose any prayer, any verse that appeals to you. Recite it as many times as you can, till it becomes a part of your unconscious mind.

3. Grow in this awareness: God is the Supreme Power that rules this Universe. God is protecting us, God is leading us, God is

guiding us, God is watching us, God is watching over us; then why should we worry? Why should we fear anything? We must make prayer a habit. Unlike all other habits, it should become integral to our daily living.

4. Set aside at least one day in a month for prayer, and prayer alone! On that day, we should forget all other mundane work and devote ourselves fully to the presence of God and pray for His benedictions. On that blessed day, we should try to wake up early in the morning, and start off the day with a little chat – a soulful, intimate, heart-to-heart talk with God.

It is often difficult to wake up early, but once we have decided to devote the day to God and experience His Divine Power, then it will be easy to pull ourselves out from bed.

Tell Him, "You are not far from me, You are with me. O God, I was fast asleep throughout the night, it is You, who have taken care of me. Today is a new dawn, a new day and I know that You will take care of me throughout the day." Then wash your face and sit in silence and chant the Divine Name or a *sloka* from a scripture or any soulful prayer. Meditate on what you recite.

The next thing is to thank God, for what He has given you. God who is ever kind and merciful has given us so much. Counting His blessings, we must thank Him. "Thank You, O Lord, thank You for everything." After the thanksgiving prayer, read a few pages from a scripture. This helps us in establishing a strong link with God. Choose any scripture, Gita, *Sukhmani, Japji Sahib, Upanishads* or Gurudev Sadhu Vaswani's *Nuri Granth.* Pick up those verses which touch your soul and then read the verses carefully, ponder over them and internalise them. After this, think about the jobs you have to do during the day, make a list of the things you have to do. Seek help from God. Seek His blessings, so that you do the job well. Be aware of God's Presence. Things done with the awareness of the Divine Presence are done effortlessly and they are always done well. Be in constant communion with God. While talking on the phone or mobile, while cooking in the kitchen or working on the computer, seek God's Divine Power and blessings. Be aware that you are bonding with the Divine Power and seeking blessings for all that you are doing, and also seeking His benedictions for the people with whom you are working or living.

5. Spread the sunshine of these blessings all

around you. Therefore, offer the loving service of your heart to those in need of comfort and help. Offer solace to a suffering person, do your bit to feed the hungry and clothe the naked of this sad world, and do not forget to feed the animals and birds; for they too, are our younger brothers and sisters in the One family of Creation. Make your love universal. With this attitude to life, you are sure to experience miracles. You will feel at peace within, which is akin to *ananda,* pure bliss.

In the rush of life and its mundane activities, we tend to forget the Divine Presence around us. We do not make God real in our life. As a result, we go astray. It is our ignorance that causes us to imagine that God has abandoned us. The fact is that it is we who have abandoned Him, kept Him away from our lives. We have to be firm in our faith. We have to remember Him every moment of our life, we have to bond with God and experience His Presence.

The practise of this day of prayer for just one day in a month, will bring peace and harmony in our life and our life will become beautiful. There will be no room for doom and gloom and pessimism and depression in such a life!

Chapter - XI

Viswarupa Darsana Yoga

In this chapter, aptly called "The Yoga of the Vision of the Cosmic Form", Arjuna is blessed with the vision of Krishna's transfiguration, he beholds the Lord's cosmic form, as *Paramatma* and *Purushottama*, the Supreme One.

The word *viswa* means 'universe'; *rupa* means 'form'. The Lord appears to Arjuna in His Cosmic Form incorporating the entire universe in His Divine Self. Arjuna cannot behold this magnificent cosmic vision with his human eyesight. Therefore, the Lord bestows *divya drishti* or a super-vision on him temporarily.

What happens in this chapter

Having heard the Lord's glories from the Lord Himself, Arjuna now asks his Divine Charioteer to reveal to him His Cosmic Form. With devotion and reverence and deep humility, he says:

> If Thou thinkest, O Lord, that by me It can be seen, then reveal to me, O Lord of Yoga (Krishna), Thine Imperishable Self. [XI:4]

The Lord grants Arjuna his wish; He also makes it possible for Arjuna to behold His *Viswarupa* with his inner, divine eye. This is how Sanjaya describes that ecstatic vision that Arjuna beheld, which in turn, it was also Sanjaya's privilege to behold, with the special perception granted to him by Ved Vyasa.

> Could but a thousand suns blaze forth all at once in the sky, it would be like the splendour of that exalted Being. [XI:12]

The vision is uplifting, wonderful and truly awe-inspiring. Arjuna sees the vast universe existing and resting in the Lord. He sees indeed, that the Lord is without any beginning, middle or end, an infinite power, with endless forms. He sees creation and destruction taking place simultaneously. He sees Divine radiance that is limitless. He prostrates before the Divine vision, and salutes the Lord in all His glory.

The Lord instils in Arjuna the incontrovertible fact that the destruction of his enemies will come about whether or not Arjuna takes part in the war, for such is the Will of the Lord. Therefore, Arjuna must stand up and fight.

> Arise thou, then! Obtain renown!
> Fight thou Thy foes!
> The kingdom awaits thee.
> By Me — Not thee — they all are slain:
> Seem thou to slay!
> Be thou My instrument!
> But strike, O knight! [XI:33]

Arjuna is thrilled, for he "hath seen That which none hath seen before." But to comfort him and allay his fear, Sri Krishna resumes His familiar, gentle human form, so that Arjuna may be reassured.

Rare and hard indeed, is it for ordinary mortals to behold the form that Arjuna has thus far beheld. No amount of scriptural study or sacrifices or by gifts or austerity, can one be entitled to behold the Form Supreme. What is required is pure and unalloyed devotion.

But by devotion to Me alone, devotion undivided, may I thus be known and seen in essence, and entered into, O Arjuna!

Who doeth work for Me, who maketh Me his supreme goal, he, My devotee, freed from attachment, without ill-will towards any creature, he cometh unto Me, O Arjuna! [XI:54-55]

Rightly did Sri Shankaracharya call this last *sloka*, "the essence of the whole Gita".

Think About it...

Arjuna has been Sri Krishna's friend, companion and cousin; and yet, it is only on the battlefield of Kurukshetra that he is afforded the opportunity to behold the Cosmic Vision or *Viswarupa darsana* of the Lord.

The Lord has prepared him for this, by teaching him the truth about the *atman,* the nature of the *jivatman* and the origin and destruction of all created things. It is only after this secret doctrine is revealed to him, that he is ready to behold the Cosmic Vision.

This glorious vision is not for mortal eyes. Krishna grants him *divya chakshu* or the Divine sight by means of which Arjuna beholds the Lord as the vast Cosmic Manifestation. The vision is at once all-comprehensive and simultaneous. In every direction Arjuna sees the Lord as the entire universe. All the created worlds, gods, beings, creatures and things animate and inanimate stand revealed as the one magnificent Form of the Lord.

Arjuna also beholds the great cosmic drama set in motion and controlled by the all-mighty power of the Lord. It is His Will alone that prevails in all things and actions, both good and bad. The Lord exhorts him to fight, for he, Arjuna is only an apparent cause of the destruction of his enemies.

Arjuna is at once ecstatic, enthralled and overwhelmed by the vision. It is the kind of expansion of consciousness that few of us are ever given to experience. Unable to withstand the power and the strain of this experience, Arjuna begs the Lord to assume once again, His usual, familiar, well loved Form.

Krishna reiterates that this vision cannot be had through any amount of austerities, study, sacrifices or philanthrophic acts. Supreme devotion is the only means by which one can have access to His grand vision.

For Your Reflection

Sri Ramakrishna Paramahansa related the following story to illustrate the magnificence of Brahman, the Supreme Self.

A fabulous monarch, wealthy beyond words, powerful beyond imagination, lived in a glorious palace, behind the seven walled gates of a great city. A visitor who was travelling through the land was fascinated to hear about him and desired intensely to see him. He was given permission to enter the King's city, and was escorted through each of the seven gates in turn. At each gate he saw a royal representative, the presiding officer of that particular gate. Each one of them was more magnificent to behold than the last. The visitor was so enthralled by each one of them, that he kept on asking, "Is this the King?" Each time he asked this question, he received the same answer, "No, this is not the King."

When he arrived at the seventh gate and was admitted into the King's palace, he saw the glorious figure of the King seated in all his splendour on the throne. The King was more wonderful, more magnificent to behold than all the rest. The man became speechless with wonder and awe; he did not have to ask questions any more; he had seen the

King; he knew now that this was indeed the King.

In this utterly simple yet profound parable, the seven gates represent the seven levels of existence. At each 'gate' we have to leave behind a lower level of existence and consciousness to enter into the highest state, the realm of pure spiritual entity. Here, only the Real and the Absolute remains, and we behold the Supreme Self face to face.

Questions:

1. We often say that God is Omnipresent, Omnipotent and Omniscient. Have you ever really thought about what exactly these oft-used words signify?

2. We have been told, earlier in the Gita, that a spark of the same Divinity also resides in us. Have you ever realised the *shakti* that is hidden in each one of us?

3. What efforts can we make, in our embodied human condition, to realise the true nature of the self, the *Atman* within us? What specifically, can you do to grow in this consciousness?

Exercises:

We are created by God, and we carry a fragment of His Divine Spirit within us. But we cannot become

God-like, until we strive to shape ourselves in His image. Despite external appearances and difficult conditions, our true nature is potentially Divine. When we realise this, there is nothing more to be said, nothing. Thus, Adi Shankara tells us in his *Vivekachudamani*:

> I cannot express by words, nor even contemplate by mind, this wealth that I have found in the ocean of the Supreme Brahman, which is full of the nectar of bliss. My mind has become merged in that ocean of bliss and is at rest... Now I am filled with that ever-blissful *Atman*.

Can we really understand God?

God is the goal of life. And God is to be realised, not merely understood or talked about. Long have we chanted hymns and recited from the scriptures and rung temple-bells and offered unending prayers, while our minds have strayed afar. Long have we kept God out of our lives. It is time to call Him in.

There is a beautiful picture by a great artist, Holman Hunt. In the picture, Christ is seen standing in a garden holding a lantern in one hand and with the other, knocking on a door. A friend of the artist said to him, "Holman, you have made a mistake. The door you have painted does not have a handle."

"It is not a mistake," answered the artist. "For this is the door of the human heart and can only be opened from inside!"

To move Godward, we need to get up and open the door and let God in. This happens only when man realises the need for God. Out of the very depths of his heart, there awakes the cry, "I have need of You, Lord! I cannot live without You!"

This is known as spiritual awakening. Something happens deep within you and your life becomes new. You are filled with light and warmth, joy and peace. You realise that the life you had lived until then, a life of creature comforts and of pride, pelf, power, was not life at all. You exclaim with Tolstoy, "To know God is to love!"

Chapter - XII

Bhakti Yoga

This chapter is simply entitled, "The Yoga of Devotion". We hear the Lord telling Arjuna about the Path of Devotion, and the true *bhakta* who is the beloved of the Lord.

This is one of the shortest chapters of the Gita. Sri Krishna chooses to teach Arjuna about *bhakti*, by outlining the qualities of His true *bhakta*. Thus this chapter becomes a manual of ideal living, appropriate conduct and right attitude for those who aspire for true devotion. A *bhakta*, according to the Lord, is so sensitive to others, that he cannot bear the suffering of others. He shows no hatred or animosity; he has no enemies. He is unmoved by praise or blame. He is ever ready to help everyone in need. He is aware that service to humanity is service to the Lord Himself. He looks upon joy and sorrow with utter equanimity. Such a devotee is indeed an ideal human being in this imperfect world of ours.

What happens in this chapter

Chapter XII is perhaps the most well-known and most discussed section in the Gita. It shows us the Path of Devotion which each one of us can choose to walk, if we so aspire.

Which is better, Arjuna wonders, to worship Sri Krishna with *bhakti,* as the Lord manifest, or to concentrate on the Unmanifest? In the worship of Krishna, both devotion and work can be offered to the Lord (i.e. *bhakti* and *seva*). But in the worship of the Unmanifest, there is only contemplation. Which is the better way of attainment for the aspirant?

The Lord avers that *Gnana Yoga* is more difficult than *Bhakti Yoga*.

> Greater is the toil of those whose minds are set on the Unmanifested; for the path of the Unmanifested is hard for the embodied to attain.   [XII:5]

But there is hope for all of us; the path of *bhakti* or devotion is open to us. All it requires is that we focus unswervingly on the Lord — fix our minds on Him, consecrate all our actions to Him and remember Him constantly. If this is not possible, we must simply choose to serve Him in all our actions. If this too, is difficult, we can simply surrender all our actions to the Lord, renouncing the fruits of such actions. "I am not the doer, Thou Art the Doer," becomes our attitude to all work.

The Lord then gives us the attributes and qualities which make a devotee dear to Him. These are outlined in the last eight verses of this Chapter, which are described as the Gita *Amritashtam* – i.e. the nectar of the Gita, in eight *slokas. Before* the evening *satsang* in the Sadhu Vaswani Mission, we hear these eight *slokas* in the divine, melodious, mellifluous voice of my Beloved Master, Gurudev Sadhu Vaswani.

What are the qualities of the true *bhakta* who is dear to the Lord?

*   He is free from ill-will and egoism. He bears no ill-will to any creature; he is forgiving, and is poised in pain and pleasure.

*   He is content and ever in harmony, his mind and understanding dedicated to the Lord.

*   He does not disturb the world, nor is he disturbed by the world.

* He is without ambition and free from passion and fear.

* He does not rejoice, grieve or crave for anything.

* He is the same to foe and friend. He is the same in honour and dishonour; he is free from attachment.

* He takes praise and blame alike. He is satisfied with whatever the Lord is pleased to grant him.

They, verily, who worship this *dharma* (law) of immortality, as taught herein, and, endowed with faith, believe in Me as the Supreme, they, My *bhaktas*, are My beloved. [XII:20]

Think About it...

Most of our sages and saints assure us that the path of *atma saakshatkaram* or self-realisation is a difficult, long drawn out process, which is not recommended to ordinary men and women; but the ever-merciful Lord does not mean the rest of us to languish without a chance of liberation. Therefore, He recommends the easy way that most of us can take to reach Him, the path of Devotion.

Although we may find it difficult to put into practice the qualities of the ideal *bhakta* outlined by Sri Krishna in this chapter, as seekers on the path, we can begin with simple exercises like repetition of the Name Divine, *kirtan* and meditation which can take us forward on the path. Constant engagements in *pooja* and *seva* also purify the mind: offering flowers to the deity, lending a helping hand to our fellow human beings, showing kindness to those in distress, reading from the sacred scriptures, listening to stories from the great *puranas,* all these activities help to cleanse and purify the mind, and sow the seeds of *bhakti yoga* in us.

For Your Reflection

The name of Prahalada is synonymous with the true bhakta. *In fact, his life story makes us wonder if a true* bhakta *is born or made.*

When Prahlada was in the womb of his mother Leelavati, it was a boon to mother and the unborn child, that they were left in the care of Maharishi Narada, in his ashram. *For Prahlada's father, the* rakshasa King Hiranyakashipu *was at that time attempting a severe* tapasya *seeking a personal boon from Sri Brahmadeva. Maharishi Narada's ashram had the most amazing environment, redolent with the fragrance of devotion. The Maharishi himself was constantly uttering the Narayana mantra with every breath. Even the wild animals in the vicinity of the ashram, so we are told, had become creatures of ahimsa, with the snake and the vulture, the lambs and the lions co-existing in peaceful harmony. This was undoubtedly due to the* taposhakti *of Maharishi Narada. Living in such an environment, Leelavati too, was steeped in the spirit of devotion, and good thoughts and good words filled her life and her consciousness. Whenever the Maharishi was free, he would narrate stories from the* puranas *to his disciples; the mother would listen for a while and then nod off, as she was often tired and sleepy. But the unborn infant in her womb was so enthralled by* the divine stories of Hari and Hari-bhakti, that he listened to the stories in rapt attention, even urging the story teller with the encouraging sounds made by all of us when we are listening to such tales!

Thus, even before Prahlada was born, he had obtained gnana upadesh from one of the greatest devotees, dearly beloved of the Lord.

A pregnant lady is described as dauhrudi (one with two hearts beating inside her). Our shastras state that all the good that she hears, thinks and utters, has a redoubled effect on the infant in her womb. Therefore, our grandmothers would insist that young pregnant women in the family should make it a habit to listen to discourses and harikathas, so that it might have a beneficial effect on the unborn infants in their wombs. So it happened with her son, who would be known to posterity as bhakta Prahlada. Prahlada was born a great Hari-bhakta and a dharmatma.

As we know, Hiranyakashipu was successful in his tapasya; Brahmadeva was forced to appear before him, and grant the desired boon; of course, the demon King's wish to become deathless, could not be granted; but Brahmadeva was forced to concede to his alternative demand: "Grant me this boon, O Lord," prayed the rakshasa, "I must not meet death either on land, in water, in fire, in air, or in the sky;

by animals or humans or devas or demons; by any weapons, during day or night. Also I must become more powerful than Indra and become the Master of triloka."

To say that Brahmadeva was taken aback would be an understatement. He blessed the demon King, and advised him to use his God-given intelligence to live well. But even though Hiranyakashipu was the son of the great Maharishi Kashyapa, he was driven by his ego and gave in to arrogance and vanity. He used his new-found power to commit every form of adharma; he tortured sadhus and sages; he harassed the virtuous and the pious. He began to act as if he were God. He even insisted that he should be worshipped by the people of his kingdom. On pain of death, people were forbidden to utter the name of Hari.

To his chagrin, one brave soul in his kingdom dared to stand up against his injunctions. This was none other than his own son, Prahlada, whose mind and heart and soul were filled with devotion to Hari. He refused to be cowed down by his father's threats and coercion; the Name of Hari was on his lips constantly.

Vinaasa kaale vipharita buddhi is a popular saying: those whose destruction is approaching, often tend to behave in the most bizarre manner.

Hiranyakashipu was so incensed by his son's Hari bhakti that he put the little boy through the most excruciating torture. Prahlada was thrown down from cliffs: he was sent to be stamped to death by wild elephants; his father even attempted to have the boy thrown into a fire to burn him alive; and cast away into the ocean to drown to his death. But the child was a true devotee of the Lord; and true to his role as deenabandhu Sri Hari saved him from all the compounded evil and multiple tortures inflicted by his cruel father.

At long last, losing his temper absolutely, the irate demon King demanded that his son should call upon his Hari to appear before him. "Where is your Hari?" he thundered. "I have looked for Him in heaven and earth and He has hidden away from me. I dare Him to show His face to me. Where is He?"

Prahlada replied "Don't doubt it at all; He is here, He is there, He is everywhere. Why do you have to go searching for Him? Wherever you look for Him with bhakti, He is sure to be there".

In great wrath, Hiranyakashipu beat the pillars in his palace shouting, "Is He here? Tell me, is He here?"

Then it was that Mahaavishnu appeared from the pillar in his Fourth Incarnation, in the form of Narasimha, the man-lion; observing Brahmadeva's boon in letter and spirit, the Lord placed Hiranyakashipa on His knees, on the threshold, and tore the demon king to pieces using no other weapons but his sharp nails!

In the darkness of his ignorance, Hiranyakashipu had imagined that he was more powerful than the Lord and that Brahma's boon had made him indestructible. He failed to take into account the Lord's might and power; his arrogance only led to his downfall!

Prahlada became known as the perfect devotee; neither pain nor threats, neither torture nor fear of death affected him in the least. He thought only of his Hari; and the Lord took care of His devotee!

Questions:

1. What do you understand by *bhakti*? How is *bhakti* to be practised?

2. What is it that you seek from the Lord as a devotee?

3. How strong is your faith in the Lord? Are you disturbed by things that seem to go against your will?

4. Have you ever complained against God or felt bitter about His 'unfair' treatment meted out to you?

Exercises:

Our sages have identified different stages by which one may attain *bhakti.* This requires certain spiritual practices.

1. *Shravana* – listening. For the aspirant, *satsang* is vital, because it enables him to listen to the voice of enlightened ones, to readings from the scriptures. Listening to *satvishaya* (good teachings) repeatedly, sets him on the spiritual path easily.

2. *Kirtan* – (singing) is the next step. I have always maintained that singing the Name Divine is the shortest route to God. Chaitanya Mahaprabhu was a great exponent of this practise.

3. *Smarana* – (constant remembrance) of the Lord is the next step. In this stage, you become aware of the Divine presence in everything you do or say; you feel His presence in every breath you take. Your life is enfolded in His presence.

4. *Archana* – (offering flowers) is not just a ritual. Symbolically, it implies that we offer good qualities, virtues like humility, compassion and goodness to the Lord.

5. *Padasevana* – (serving the feet) symbolises the spirit of service. This is what Gurudev Sadhu Vaswani meant, when he described service of the poor as the best form of worship to God.

6. *Vandana* – (bowing down) within the heart, the devotee reveres the Lord; outwardly, he reveres all creatures, all objects which are, after all, manifestations of the Divine.

7. *Atmanivedana* – is absolute surrender. This is the ultimate goal of spiritual attainment, to live in total surrender to the Lord.

Bhakti Yoga – the path of devotion to the Lord – is in essence, the path of love – love that is unconditional, whole-hearted, selfless and completely fulfilling. Alas, human love is frittered away on worldly objects and goals that are perishable, mortal and therefore, utterly futile. But when our love is bestowed on God, we will find complete and absolute fulfilment. We will learn to transcend the ego, and commune with the Divine.

Chapter - XIII

Kshetra Kshetrajna Vibhaga Yoga

This title is translated as "The Yoga of Distinction between the Field and the Knower of the Field". Gurudev Sadhu Vaswani referred to this chapter as "The Philosophy of Life" expounded by Sri Krishna, a rock on which Arjuna may build his destiny. It is a philosophy of life which can help us in our quest after the Perfect Life.

"This body is called the *Kshetra,* O Kaunteya, and the wise refer to him who knows as the *Kshetrajna,*" the Lord tells Arjuna. Scholars also refer to this 'distinction' as the discrimination that teaches us the difference between outer form and inner life, matter and spirit.

What happens in this chapter

This is regarded by many scholars as one of the most complex and mystical as well as one of the most illuminating chapters of the Gita.

By drawing our attention to the distinction between *Prakriti* and *Purusha* (Nature and the Spirit), the field and the knower of the field – i.e. *Kshetra* the body, or the scene of activity; and *Kshetrajna* or consciousness, the Lord also reveals to us the nature of the working of this Universe.

"Know Me, Arjuna, as the Omnipresent *Kshetrajna* who abides in all *Kshetras;* and the Knowledge of these two is deemed by Me as true Knowledge," the Lord tells His disciple. Whatever we see around us is a combination of *Purusha* and *Prakriti,* spirit and matter, soul and body. In creation and in evolution *Prakriti* is said to be the cause, while for the experience of pleasure and pain *Purusha* is the cause. The Lord Himself is the knower of the body, who dwells in all bodies. He who realises that the body is the field, and the indweller in the body is the Lord, has attained real wisdom. The Fields may be different, but the Knower of the Field is one. The individual souls *(jivatmas)* are different but the Supreme Soul, *Paramatma* is One only. As the one Sun illumines the whole world, so does the Lord of the *Kshetra* illumine the whole *Kshetra*.

The constituents of the field *(kshetra)* are 24 principles:

1. The *avyakta* or the unmanifest;

2. The *ahankara* or the ego;

3. *Buddhi* or reason;

4. *Manas* or mind – the discursive reason;

5.-14. The five sense organs for acquiring knowledge and the domains of these senses (eye – sight; ears – hearing; nose – smell; skin – touch; tongue-taste;)

15.-19. The five operative senses — voice, hands, legs and the reproductive and excretory organs;

20.-24. Five gross elements or *pancha bhutas* – i.e. earth, fire, water, air and ether.

These are also the twenty-four constituent principles of which the body is formed.

Vikaras or modifications arise in the *kshetra,* because our *jiva* is associated with *maya.* These *vikaras* are desire, aversion, pleasure and pain, association, cognition and constancy.

In human nature, there are two forces at work, one leading the soul towards God, and the other towards ignorance. The individual soul, who is ignorant of the *Atman* or *Purusha,* identifies himself with the body, and is subject to the three *gunas.* But one who is aware of the Spirit Supreme, sees the Supreme Self in all; he dedicates his life to the Lord and attains liberation.

Freedom and immortality are assured to us when we realise that the One Imperishable Spirit dwells equally in all perishable forms. In this awareness, we perceive that *prakriti* is responsible for all activities, while the *Atman* is actionless.

> They who, by the eye of wisdom, see this distinction between the field and the Knower of the field, and (who understand) how beings may be released from *Prakriti,* liberated from matter, they verily, go to the Supreme. [XIII:34]

Think About it...

The distinction between matter and spirit outlined in this chapter is called the Supreme Reality. And, the Lord tells us, he who knows this Supreme Reality is instantly liberated.

The physical body of man is constituted of the same combination of elements which constitute this Universe. What we must understand now is the true nature of the *Atman* and how and why it is associated with this matter. People who do not understand this important distinction are afflicted with *Dehathma Bramam* (the illusion that the body is the *Atman*) and are doomed to suffer in worldly life as bonded individuals. Once we understand this distinction, Self Realisation becomes possible.

For Your Reflection

The Supreme Self or Paramatman *is the Indweller in all the* jivatmas. *He who is aware that the Supreme Self inhabits all forms of creation, needs to know nothing more; he becomes a Realised Soul.*

How can we imbibe and internalise this awareness? It is not easy. "Some through meditation behold the Atman *in their self by their own self; others experience It through the* Yoga of Knowledge *and still others through the* Yoga of Action," *the Lord tells Arjuna. "Yet others, not knowing Him thus, worship Him as they have heard from others."*

Who will teach us this Supreme Truth?

Adi Shankara himself needed to be taught this Supreme reality! Let me narrate to you the well-known incident from his life, which has come down to us in many versions, many interpretations, but captures the essence of his life and teaching.

Early one morning Shankara was returning from the river Ganga, where he had just taken a holy dip. In his sannyasin's kamandala *(water-pot) he was carrying the sacred* Gangajal *with which he would perform his daily* pooja. *In the dark hours before the dawn, he found his path obstructed by a huge, bulky figure of a* Chandaala, *an outcast. Impulsively,*

174

he cried out: "Gaccha, Gaccha! *Move away! Move away!"*

Without moving an inch, the figure seen in the semi-darkness retorted: "What do you want to be removed? What do you want to remove — and from what? Is it my body that you consider impure, and wish to remove from your vicinity? Is it my consciousness that you wish to remove from your consciousness? Does not the sun reflect its brilliance in the sacred waters of the Ganga, as well as the impure waters of the gutter in the public garden? Is there any difference, therefore, in the Sun?"

Indeed, these are not questions to be answered in a conventional sense. Sri Shankara, one of our greatest Masters, feels a sense of tremendous revelation. He falls at the feet of the figure who obstructs his path and utters the simple statement: "He who experiences this is my Guru."

We know it was the Lord of Varanasi, Lord Visweswara, Lord Shiva Himself, who thus accosted Sri Shankara. God Himself assumed the form of the Guru to remind Sri Shankara that He is also the Indweller within us all. The story goes on to tell us that as Sri Shankara prostrates himself before the Lord, the Lord bent down to enfold him in His arms: a deeply symbolic act which signifies that the God, the Guru and the Incarnate Soul are One.

Questions:

1. Is not this the role of the Guru, to give a meaning to our life? To make us understand what we really are and our true nature?

2. If Sri Shankara needed such a one, can ordinary mortals like us do without a Guru to lead us towards the Light?

3. True, the light of the *Paramatman* shines within each one of us: but alas, we live in the outer darkness, unaware of the Light within. What can we do to become conscious of the indwelling Light?

Exercises:

Let me repeat, the Light inextinguishable dwells within each one of us, but we cannot see it, for it is hidden behind veils of ignorance, veils of mind and matter. The great wall of the ego stands between us and the *Paramatman,* and we cannot see the Light Divine. It is the Guru who can destroy the great wall of the ego and lead us from darkness to light.

Sri Ramakrishna gave us the incomparable parable of the ten water pots reflecting the sun. We look at the ten suns and we realise there can be only one which is real. So we break one of the pots. Now there are nine reflected suns and one real sun. We break eight of the pots, one after the other. Now one real sun remains, along with just one reflected sun. We break the last pot, and only the real sun remains. Can we describe that which remains? Can we even see it with our naked eyes? "What is, remains," Sri Ramakrishna explains. "The reflected sun makes us realise that there is indeed a real sun."

Breaking the water pots is symbolic of eliminating each element in the Universe until we realise where the Light comes from. This is discrimination that is hard-earned.

The "Third Eye", the Inner Eye of the Spirit remains closed for most of us, its vision impaired by our bad *karma.* The cataract of the ego, the veils of arrogance and pride, have covered this inner eye completely. The Guru is the 'eye' surgeon, who can restore our inner vision.

Why do we need the Guru? The Guru is the great cleanser, a great purifier – not merely a great teacher. Caught in the web of *maya,* caught in the snare of sensual desires and worldly pleasures, we accumulate bad *karma,* birth after birth after birth.

Alas, our poor efforts are not enough to cleanse these impurities. But the Guru's grace can cleanse us and lead us towards the Divine Light of God.

The Guru reaches out to us and with his grace, annihilates the ego; he tears away the veils of ignorance which shield us from self-realisation; he reveals our true identity to us – *Tat Twamasi!* That art Thou! It is his grace that liberates us from bondage to the circle of life and death. This gift of Grace has devolved on the Guru from God Himself – for God knows that the world is in dire need of Grace. His Presence is of course Universal: He gives us the Guru, for our individual benefit, for our personal liberation. This is why our ancient scriptures enjoin us to venerate the Guru as God:

> *Gurur Brahma, Gurur Vishnu*
> *Gurur Devo Maheshwara…*

In this human birth, we cannot see God in person; but it is our good fortune that we can see the Guru, hear his *upadesh,* associate ourselves with daily *satsang,* accept his gracious *prasad* – indeed, grasp his holy feet firmly and through him, all God's blessings and all God's grace will come to us!

In India, we speak of *tattva gnana* (philosophical wisdom) as well as *tattva darshana* (philosophical vision). Even such a vision is offered to us, when we behold a realised Soul, face to face.

It can be a truly transforming vision!

It is this *darshana* of truth that our ancient seers and sages sought and obtained. This is how the *rishis* of the *Upanishad* describe the mystery of the Guru and his *tattva darshana:*

> Without learning it from another, how could one know that?
>
> But to hear it from just any man is not sufficient,
>
> Even should he repeat it a hundred or a thousand times...
>
> Neither through reasoning, nor through idea,
>
> Nor even through simple recitation of the Vedas, can one know it...
>
> Worthy of admiration is he who speaks it,
>
> Worthy of admiration is he who hears it,
>
> Worthy of admiration is he who knows it having been well taught.   [Katha Upanishad]

To be conscious of this, is to be One with the Divine. It is emancipation from the bondage of matter; it is liberation from the delusion that springs from the attachments and contact with the world.

This, the Gita describes as *"brahmistiti"* – Divine state. This state, we can reach, only under the guidance of an illumined one, a sage.

The Guru creates us anew. We are reborn in the spirit, when we surrender to him. He is much more than an 'instructor', 'adviser' or 'professor'. He is an enlightener with a transforming power. Spirituality is, as we have seen, a tremendous *shakti.* And the Guru's *shakti* lies in this, that he leads forth the disciple not only towards liberation, but towards himself, so that the disciple becomes a teacher in his own right.

Therefore do we revere the Guru as the "Light-bringer". His words of wisdom, his *bani,* charged with divine and holy meaning, enter the heart and shine there as jewels bright; they lead the disciple to the Presence Divine. The Guru's words are the disciple's torch in darkness, they are the disciple's source of true happiness in the strife of this broken life.

In the great adventure that is life, God and man are comrades – although, in his ignorance, man often fails to perceive His divine connections. He is a part of the great Universal Spirit – however, it is hidden from his eyes. God is invisible to man. We are unable to see Him, feel Him, touch Him, speak to Him and hear His sweet voice.

Let me assure you: we can see Him, we can feel His presence, we can commune with Him one-to-one. The Guru can help us achieve this communion if we hand ourselves over to his care.

It was a Sufi *dervish* who said: "You must meet God everyday. And if you cannot meet Him, go and meet someone who has met Him and who lives in constant communion with Him. The two are not separate from each other!"

Chapter - XIV

Guna Traya Vibhaga Yoga

This is translated as "The Yoga of the Differentiation of the Three Qualities". Gurudev Sadhu Vaswani referred to this chapter also as "The Conquest of the Three Qualities".

The three qualities referred to are *sattva, rajas* and *tamas* – i.e. purity/holiness; action/drive; laziness/inertia. In this chapter, the Lord gives us the supreme wisdom regarding the conquest of these three *gunas* recognised by contemporary psychology as constituents of the human psyche.

What happens in this chapter

Having learnt that Nature *(Prakriti)* is the Field through which the Supreme Self *(Purusha)* gives expression to itself, we now learn a little more about the qualities *(gunas)* of nature – what they are, how they bind man, how they operate and how we may rise above them.

The three *gunas* are *sattva, rajas,* and *tamas,* purity, passion and inertia. All of them bind us through attachment. The essentially immortal *Atman* becomes bound to this mortal frame of life, through the action of the *gunas.* And this means that as long as we are so bound, the cycle of *karma,* birth and death will continue.

Tamas, the darkest and lowest of the three, is born of ignorance, causes delusion and binds one strongly with miscomprehension, laziness and excessive sleep. *Rajas* is passion, and gives rise to ambition, *trishna* or desire, and impulse to action. It binds one by creating attachment to action. *Sattva* is lofty, holy and pure; but it does not lead to liberation. As the Lord points out, "*Sattva* is stainless, luminous and free from evil; it binds one through attachment to happiness and attachment to *gnana* (knowledge)".

Although *Sattva* is superior to the others, the reality is that each of the three *gunas* can be powerful enough to subdue and dominate over the other qualities at varying times and conditions. Thus, we are told that at different moments, on different occasions, one or the other quality dominates our action and thought.

Whichever quality out of the *trigunas* is predominant at the time of one's death will determine the next birth one will take.

Of these *tamas,* born of ignorance, can be conquered by *karma yoga* or right action; *rajas,* the source of which is thirst for sensual pleasure, can be cured by dedication to one's own duty or *swadharma; sattva,* which is itself stainless and pure, nevertheless binds us to happiness, and must be conquered by desireless detachment.

The *gunatita* or one who has conquered the three *gunas,* is firmly rooted in the Supreme Self. He is desireless, he is unaffected by praise or blame; he is the same to friend and enemy; he sees God in all, and regards himself as the instrument of the Lord.

He who serveth Me with unswerving devotion, passes beyond the *gunas* and becomes one with Brahman.

For I am the abode of Brahman, the inexhaustible nectar of immortality: (I am the ground) of Eternal Righteousness and (the source) of unending Bliss.

[XIV:26-27]

Think About it...

"Conquer the three *gunas* Arjuna!" the Lord tells his dear, devoted disciple. "Be a seer!"

It is essential for us to understand the three *gunas* and their relation to the human personality. It is only when we have understood them that we can conquer them, rise above them and thus advance on the spiritual path.

When darkness and inertia predominate, you have a sure sign that *tamas* prevails. The *tamasic* man manifests negative qualities such as anger, greed, falsehood, violence, deception, hypocrisy, languor, discord, grief, delusion, gloom, wretchedness, sleep, negative expectation, fear and inactivity—this is according to Srimad Bhagavat Purana.

These negative qualities are obviously hindrances on the path of spiritual evolution. But they also impede progress and personality development in earthly life! Therefore, when expressions of *tamas* impede our progress, we must remove them from our personality.

Rajas is the child of strong desire and attachment. When greed, extreme ambition and restless activity predominates our life, it means that *rajas* prevails. In fact the man of *rajas* is marked by a zeal for work.

The man of *rajas* is always in the midst of struggle and work. He has a strong desire to assert and achieve. He struggles hard to show, to establish his superiority over others. He goes about in life, not as the servant of the Lord, but imagining himself to be the Lord of all he surveys. The man under the influence of *rajas* is the man of action, of initiative, of inordinate ambition and restlessness.

The *rajasic* man is thus characterised by the following: restless activity, uncontrolled desires and various impurities of the mind. According to Srimad Bhagavata, the following qualities are expressions of *rajas:* desire, lust, selfish activity, pride, craving, rigidity, stubbornness, creating disharmony, indulgence in sense pleasures, love of fame and pride, excessive attachment, frivolity, selfish exertion and egotistical strength.

Sattva is the principle of truth, beauty and harmony. The Srimad Bhagavata tells us that *sattva* manifests itself in the quality of serenity, self-control, austerity, truthfulness, compassion, endurance, pure memory, contentment, renunciation, non-covetousness, faith, repugnance for sin, etc.

Sri Krishna also mentions those qualities associated with *sattva:* fearlessness, purity of mind, steadfastness, control of the senses, sacrifice, study of the scriptures, non-violence, truthfulness, freedom from anger and freedom from envy, malice and pride.

Sattva elevates the mind, expanding our consciousness. The *buddhi* becomes radiant, and the whole personality becomes vital and joyous. One is able to rise above the narrow, restricting circumstances of the material world, and adopt a tranquil, serene, balanced attitude to life.

Unfortunately for many people, we are able to attain *sattva* only for a very short while. Our great spiritual elders say that when our good *karma* of the past fructifies, it manifests itself as *sattva* in our personality. At such times we become serene, joyous and tranquil; we radiate pure vitality and happiness. But when the effect of good *karma* ends, we are back in the clutches of *tamas* (dullness) and *rajas* (passion). Thus, we lose our equanimity and serenity, and we are distracted by the troubles, sufferings and sorrows of this life.

Whenever we experience true happiness, it is because *sattva* predominates in our life and character. Unable to realise this truth, we attribute happiness to external objects and circumstances. When we lose our sense of joy, we attribute it to the loss of these objects and circumstances. Whereas, if we knew the truth, we would work constantly to cultivate *sattva,* so that we may always feel true joy, the peace and bliss that surpasses understanding, and move forward on the path of liberation.

For Your Reflection

The story is told to us of a merchant who was attacked by three thieves, while he was passing through a forest. The roughest and crudest of the three beat him up severely; the second one looted him of all his possessions; the first one said to his companions, "Let us kill him and put an end to the matter." But the second rejected the idea; he tied up the merchant's hands and feet and pushed him into a deep pit, and both of them departed. However, the third one took pity on the victim. Escaping the notice of the other two, he came back, untied the man, led him out of the forest and bid him escape. The merchant thanked him profusely and begged him to accompany him to his home so that he could be rewarded. But the thief declined, and went back to join his companions.

In this story, the rough, crude thieves represent tamas and rajas; the third thief represents sattva. But the point to be noted is that even sattva, on its own, cannot lead us to our true abode. The three rogues have to be left behind; the three gunas have to be transcended, before we attain liberation.

Like the three thieves, the three gunas possess our soul, and deprive us of our spiritual treasure.

We are tied by the bonds of karma and thrown into the pit of the world process. Sattva can help to free us – it can even point to us the path of liberation, but it cannot take us to our ultimate goal! Therefore, as true seekers and aspirants, we must transmute tamas into rajas and rajas into sattva – and ultimately transcend sattva and become established in the Divine Self.

Questions:

1. What is your predominant temper or mood?
2. What are the kind of clothes you like to wear?
3. What are your preferences in food?
4. Are you aware that all of these can reflect your predominant *guna* or quality?

Exercises:

Sri Krishna tells us in the Gita:

> When the embodied soul hath crossed over the three *gunas,* whence all bodies have been produced, then, indeed, freed from birth and death, from old age and sorrow, he drinketh the waters of immortality.
>
> [XIV:20]

The Lord's message to his dear, devoted disciple is: "Conquer the three *gunas* Arjuna!" Such a man becomes a seer. He realises:

1. That liberation is won by him who knows that all work, all action, arises out of the three *gunas.*

2. That there is One beyond the *gunas,* One who is Supreme. He is higher than the *gunas.*

The wise man is one who crosses over the three *gunas,* controls them, conquers them, so that they move in rhythm and harmony with the wisdom of Krishna. Such a man is truly liberated. Gurudev Sadhu Vaswani tells us that his marks are as follows:

1. He is indifferent to the three *gunas* when they are in action, as also when they cease to act.

2. He is undisturbed by the results of action. He realises that all activity belongs to the *gunas.* He sees the *gunas* at work in himself and others, and is seated in their midst, indifferent, unconcerned. He is unshaken by the *gunas.* He is a pilgrim. As dreams do not disturb the awakened one, so *gunas* do not bind him.

3. All things and beings are states to him. Indifferent is he to *dwandas* – pairs of opposites. Therefore is he the same to friend or foe, the same in like or dislike, in censure

and praise, in misery and prosperity. To him, a clod and pebble are alike.

4. He does all his work without desire. He hath abandoned all ambition, undertaking and enterprise for selfish motives.

What is the way that a man must tread in order to cross the *gunas* and become one with the Eternal? It is the way of exclusive, unswerving devotion, and loving service to Sri Krishna.

In love, he annihilates himself and enters into union with the Lord. He becomes nothing, a zero, and is united with the Self Supreme. Such a man realises the *atmaswarupa.* He enters into Krishna, the Eternal, he becomes the Eternal.

Chapter - XV

Purushottama Yoga

The title of this chapter is translated as "The Yoga of the Supreme Person". Gurudev Sadhu Vaswani referred to it as the chapter on "The World Tree". Sri Krishna pictures the entire cosmos as an *ashvattha tree* – the cosmic World-Tree, which must be cut down by the weapon of non-attachment.

What happens in this chapter

The Lord now begins to tell Arjuna about the cosmic World-Tree, the tree of *Prakriti,* or Nature, which he describes as the *ashvattha* tree. The word *ashvattha* means "not stable" or "in a flux" – i.e. that which is constantly subject to change, even as everything in this world is subject to decay and death.

"With roots at the top (in Heaven), branches below, and with *chhandaas* (meters of vedic hymns) as its leaves stands the imperishable *ashvattha* tree," the Lord tells Arjuna. "He who knows this is *"vedavit"*, i.e., knower of the truth in the Vedas. The branches of that tree spread upwards and downwards and its shoots of sensuality *(vishaya)* sprout according to the *gunas*. The roots spread downwards into the world of humans thereby producing *karmas* and its reactions."

All trees have their roots down in the earth, but this remarkable tree of *samsara* or creation has its roots above – in the Supreme Self. The trunk and branches of this tree grow downwards, nourished by the *gunas;* sense-objects are its buds;

its secondary roots stretch down below, binding it to worldly action.

Alas, not many of us understand the real form of this tree – neither its origin, nor its end, nor its foundation. The Lord urges us to cut the tree down, by the weapon of non-attachment.

Cutting down does not mean destroying the tree; it only means that we have to detach ourselves from the cosmos; this tree can be 'uprooted' with the sharp axe of detachment from the sense objects constituted by the three *gunas*. When we do this we are released from the erroneous knowledge *(vipareetha jnanam)* that the *atman* is the same as *sariram;* and when this illusion is destroyed and the agency *(karthruthvam)* of the three *gunas* that held the pristine *atman* in bondage is understood, we are led towards *moksha* or liberation.

In this Cosmic Tree of *Prakriti* appear *jivas* or individuals. The Purushottama or the Supreme Self, pervades all; He is Indestructible and is known as the Supreme Person. He who knows the Lord as Purushottama, knoweth all and he worships the Lord with all his soul. The Lord as Purushottama pervades, sustains and rules over everything: the scient or the conscious *(chit),* the non-scient or the unconscious *(achit)* and *Prakriti* in the universe.

> Thus have I told thee the most secret teaching, Arjuna! He who knoweth this, he is illuminated and his labours are finished, O Arjuna!   [XV:20]

Think About it...

> There are two *Purushas* in the world,
>
> The mortal and Immortal One;
>
> The elements are mortal all,
>
> The highest is the Immortal One.

Two *Purushas:* These are two aspects of the individual soul, the soul in itself, and when it is associated with the objects of life, and becomes *Bhutatman, Jivatman,* or Egoism *(Ahankara).* The greatest is God, the Supreme *Purusha.*

Philosophy is defined as the rational investigation of the truths and principles of being, knowledge, or conduct. The issue of existence is the main issue of philosophy, but most of us are not even aware of our own existence. It needed a great philosopher, Descartes to say: "I think, therefore I am." For many of us, understanding existence is the same as comprehending the Ultimate Reality, which is God. This is what the Lord helps us to do here. We are; we live in this world; we experience the material existence on the physical plane; but over and beyond this physical plane of life is our connection with the Supreme Self, the Creator of all that lives. When we live in oblivion of our relationship with the Universe and the Creator, we live in the darkness of oblivion; we refuse to see the tree for the leaves; we confine ourselves to the body and become bound by the actions of the *gunas.*

For Your Reflection

The Upanishads are full of wise and profound truths.

In one of the Upanishads, the Rishi tells us of a tree on whose branches two birds were perched. The bird which sat on the uppermost branch was beautiful, calm, serene and pure, a veritable joy to behold. Further down, on a lower branch was the second bird, which appeared to be greatly agitated and forlorn. It seemed as if this bird was drowning in an ocean of distress, tossed about by a thousand fears and anxieties. Both birds seemed to be living in worlds apart, though they sat on the same tree.

Whenever the second bird looked up at the first one, it thought: "How beautiful is the bird up there! It is so joyous and serene. Will I ever attain such peace and joy?"

As this thought crossed its mind, the second bird tried to spread its wings and fly up to the topmost branch where the beautiful bird sat. It hopped from one branch to another, its wings fluttering in the effort to fly higher. And as it moved up the tree, the little bird found itself experiencing a unique feeling of joy and peace. Its heart seemed to light up with a divine radiance! The flight upwards was a wonderful experience!

But even as it attempted to fly up, the little bird felt the urge to cast its eyes down below. The lower branches were full of temptingly luscious fruits, which seemed to beckon the bird invitingly.

"Those fruits appear to be so appetising," thought the little bird. He swooped down in an instant and began to peck at the fruits. Here and there, he found the fruits were sweet and juicy; but there were quite a few which were bitter. As he tasted the sweet fruits, the little bird was elated; but when he tasted the bitter ones, he became dispirited and dejected. All the joy and peace that he had felt only moments ago, now seemed to be lost, and the little bird wept with grief and anguish.

What do you think these two birds symbolise? The radiant bird that sits on the uppermost branch is none other than Paramatman, the Lord Himself. The miserable bird, caught up in the temptation of the lower branches is jivatman, the human being.

The jivatman eats of the fruit of the tree of life; the fruits are sometimes sweet, but more often than not, they are bitter. Man considers himself happy when pleasurable experiences occur to him; he loses himself in despair, when bitter experiences confront him. When the grey clouds of grief and despair darken his horizons and he has nowhere to turn, he looks up above him, and he beholds the beautiful vision of the Higher Self. "Ah," he sighs, "When will I attain such joy and peace?"

Impelled to seek true joy and peace, he too, like the bird, attempts to spread the wings of his spirit and ascend to the Lord. But the moment his attention turns to worldly matters, the moment he looks downwards, he falls a prey to his appetites and passions, and is caught in the everlasting cycle of desire and despair.

Alas, this is the condition of many of us on this earth. We are like the bird that sits on the lower branches of the tree of life; overcome by our greed for worldly fruits, we fall a prey to our own passions and desires. For the sake of ephemeral pleasures, we sacrifice an innate radiance and peace of mind that all of us are capable of achieving, when we decide to spread our wings and fly upward.

In truth, there is no intrinsic difference between the two birds, for man's soul is but an aspect of God; the jivatman is part of the Paramatman. Man's trouble is that as jivatman, he has come into this world with a body, mind and five senses. The senses hanker after material pleasures; the mind runs after the senses; and the jivatman is dragged along by the mind. Alas, the jivatman loses sight of its own true nature, and is entrapped in the pursuit of sense-indulgence. Very occasionally, these indulgences seem to bring with them a little physical pleasure; but often, grief and frustration are the fruit of such indulgence, and the jivatman yearns for the radiance it has lost.

Many are the legends and stories that tell us of rishis and munis, who, lured by the senses, were led astray from the path of virtue. We fall a prey to temptations, even like the bird on the lower branches of the tree of life. The beautiful bird perched up above, constantly beckons us. "Come to me, and attain true joy and peace!" it calls out. But we seldom look up, nor do we listen to its insistent voice. We are slaves of our material world. We only heed the call of our own mind, which, in turn, is lured by the pleasures of the senses.

Let us make friends with our minds; let us free the mind from slavery to sense impressions; let not our mind turn into our enemy. When the mind becomes our friend, it will lead us up towards the paramatman – for Lord Krishna Himself awaits us. He is constantly watching us, and calling out to us, "You are of Me, you are of the Eternal! Do not lose sight of your real self in the darkness of maya."

Questions:

1. Reflect on the following passages:

   Make God a reality in your life. Awaken love for the Divine in your hearts. A human being without love is like a hive without honey, a flower without fragrance. Therefore, love God with your mind, heart and soul.

   Man does not live by the beats of his heart, but by the grace of God. Let our lives be rooted in the Holy Name of God, and we will discover that the human body is but a garment we have worn.

   You are not the body, you are the immortal *Atman* within. *Tat twam asi!* That art Thou!

2. What is your response to the two passages? Put your reflections down.

Exercises:

Shariram brahma mandiram, our ancient scriptures tell us. The human body is a temple of the Lord. "I dwell within every human heart," Sri Krishna assures us in the Bhagavad Gita. Just imagine, the Almighty, the Power Supreme dwells within us. Each one of us is a potent Krishna. Yet we live like weaklings. At the slightest difficulty, before the smallest obstacle, we retreat, we give way and break down. We succumb to pressures and problems, we get caught in a vicious circle of desires. It is sad, that despite the great *'Shakti'* of Krishna within us, we despair and fall into melancholy.

Gurudev Sadhu Vaswani, repeatedly urged us, 'Awaken the *shakti* within you.' He opened an *Ashram* in Rajpur and named it *'The Shakti Ashram'*. He opened another *Ashram* in South India and called it, *'Para Shakti Ashram'*. He urged the youth to be strong, to awaken the *shakti* within; to be brave and accept the challenges of life, to tap the 'power house' of infinite energy within us.

1. The first thing we must do in order to awaken this *shakti,* is to turn the mind inward, towards this power house within us. Turning inward is not easy, for our senses are constantly engaged in drawing the mind outward. Lured by the five senses, the mind roams far and wide, and begins to wander aimlessly, for these senses ignite desires, wants and needs. If only we could introspect, reflect and dwell within, even for a few minutes, we would become aware of the power within.

2. Our ancient spiritual teachers tell us: there is but one way to focus the mind inwards; and this is the way of *abhyasa,* of meditation. During meditation, our thoughts are withdrawn from external happenings and are focussed inward. Meditation stills the mind and creates space for serenity within us. The experience of meditation is so beautiful, that beginners are often reluctant to bring it to an end.

   We may begin the practice of meditation with one hour, then extend it to two hours and finally make it to three hours. If we manage to sit in meditation for three hours continuously, we experience a mystical panorama.

3. Meditation brings AWARENESS: 'I am not this physical body that I wear. I am the eternal *Atman.* My soul is not bound by this body or the senses. My life is precious. It is a gift from God, given to me for a specific purpose, a higher purpose.' When this realisation dawns on us, we rise above our lower self, the self of the ego, the self of passion and pride, of lust and hatred and greed. When we abandon this ego self, we realise the Vedic injunction: *Tat tvam asi!* That art thou!

It is our great mistake to identify ourselves with the physical body. Besides this 'ego self', we are blessed with a higher potent energy, called the higher-self, the larger-self, the true-self, which the Gita describes as The Self-Supreme. Within each one of us is the Universal Self, the self that makes us one with all that is, with the life force of this universe.

Meditation helps us to understand and experience this higher self. The higher self is *'shakti',* power unlimited and infinite. This Higher Self is indestructible. No weapon can kill it, no fire can burn it, no ocean can drown it and no wind can wipe it dry. It is Eternal.

4. Yet another practice that is highly recommended by the great masters is the practice of silence. Once you begin to practise silence, you will realise the transitory nature of human life. You will begin to ask yourself, "Who am I? What is the purpose of my life?" This is why, the *sadhana,* the discipline of going within through silence is termed as the best method of self enquiry. This is why our saints and sages and holy men urge us to meditate, for it is the way of self realisation, the way of tapping the Power within.

Some of us may find it difficult to practise meditation. The practice of silence is an easier option. Close your eyes and listen with your inner consciousness to the voice of the great Ones. Utter the Name Divine, and your favourite words from the scriptures in the silent centre of your soul. I firmly believe that a silent prayer is far more powerful than the spoken prayer. One verse from *Gurbani* which I love to hear again and again within my heart is:

O Lord, the redeemer of pain and suffering, O Father of the orphans, who breathes in every life, Nanak seeks refuge under your protection.

Reciting such verses from the holy scriptures will bond you with your Higher Self. You will keep on going deeper and deeper within, until you perceive the beautiful interior-space of your immortal soul. You will now experience the kind of peace and joy that surpass all worldly pleasures you have ever felt. You will, by now have found the power of the spirit within you.

We have passed through many lives. We have accumulated the *vasanas* of evil thoughts, words and deeds. We are imprisoned by the *karmic* bonds of our previous births, so much so that they have become the shackles of our present existence. We carry the yoke of negative *karmas* and we long to break free, like the pathetic fish caught in the snare of the trawler.

Don't let anyone tell you that escape from the snare is impossible! Liberation is yours for the asking. You can make your life anew. For man is not a creature of his destiny. He is the creator of his destiny.

If you wish to create your own destiny, you must be free of the burden of your past; you must erase the past through *Sadhana,* through the realisation of your true self. You must create a new space within, sow new thoughts of true liberation and freedom thereon. You must learn to meditate, you must go into silence; you must chant the Name of God within your heart. This will help you tap the latent power within you, it will open the reservoir of *shakti* that is deep inside your spirit. Once you experience this power, a new serenity, a vital energy will flow into your life. You will find this experience so uplifting, that you will overcome all the limitations of your physical existence, and rise above the restrictions of your external environment.

Let me repeat, you are not the pathetic weakling you take yourself to be. You are a spark of the Supreme Self. You are a child of God. His power and energy are yours. Only three things are essential to unleash the hidden power within you: (1) Silence and Meditation; (2) Self-control and Self-discipline; (3) Selfless service or giving away of oneself.

Chapter - XVI

Daivasura Sampad Vibhaga Yoga

This title is translated as "The Yoga of the Distinction between the Divine and the Demoniac". We are taught to recognise the Divine and Demoniac qualities in human beings, so that we may cultivate those divine qualities that are beloved of the Lord.

Daivi sampadi is our divine heritage, while *asura sampadi* refers to demoniac qualities. These were referred to briefly in the ninth chapter as the awakened and the deluded souls. The former are characterised by divine attributes, while the latter possess demoniac qualities. The Lord teaches us to distinguish between the two so that we may cultivate the right attributes and behaviour which are dear to the Lord.

What happens in this chapter

The Lord classifies two distinct sets of qualities which are opposed to each other, He urges us to root out our evil traits, and cultivate divine qualities. Both are to be found in human beings, for in all of us is a mixture of the three *gunas.*

Fearlessness, purity of mind, sacrifice and service, compassion and humility characterise the divine being while hypocrisy, arrogance, delusion, anger and ignorance characterise the demoniacal being.

Divine properties lead to liberation and the demoniac to bondage. Grieve not, O Arjuna, for thou art born with the divine heritage.   [XVI:5]

The divine qualities lead us Godward; as for the demoniac qualities, they open up the triple gateway of hell – lust, wrath and greed. Unless we are released from these three gates, we cannot proceed towards our highest goal.

Therefore, let the holy law be thy rule in determining what should be done or what should not be done. Knowing what hath been declared by the holy law, do thou, O Arjuna, thy work in this world.   [XVI:24]

To win release from the gates of darkness, the gates of hell, man must turn away from the promptings of desire and turn to the holy law *(shastra vidhi)*. The holy laws of the *shastras* (scriptures) show us what is right and what is wrong, for the *shastras* represent the accumulated wisdom of the ages.

Think About it...

The Lord sets out the qualities of Divine heritage in three *slokas;* while *slokas* 7-17 deal elaborately with the mind-set, attitude and culture of the demoniacal men. Why are they set out in such detail, we might wonder; it is because we must take care to cultivate those features that are dear to the Lord, and avoid the demoniacal ones in our life and actions. Swami Desika describes the former as *daivamsam* and the latter as *asuraamsam.*

The charecteristics of *daivamsam* as enumerated by the Lord are as follows:

* Fearlessness *(abhayam)* and freedom from sorrow over losing what is dear

* Purity of mind *(Satthva-samsuddhi)* characterised by the freedom from desire, anger, jealousy and deceit

* Steadfastness in knowledge and *yoga (Gnana yoga vyavastithithi); focused existence to comprehend the true nature of the Self*

* Alms giving of rightfully earned things to the righteous (*Saathvika dhanam*)

* Self-control and preventing the mind from straying into improper areas (*dhama*)

* The performance of daily *karmas (Yajna) such as Deva Yajna, Pithru Yajna, Bhutha Yajna, Manushya Yajna and Brahma Yajna*

* The study of the Vedas with the clear understanding that the subject of the scriptures is all about the Lord's glories and the ways to worship Him (*Svadhyaya*)

* Penance/austerity to detach oneself from material desires (*Tapa*)

* Uprightness; the compatibility of mind, body and speech with respect to interaction with others (*Aarjavam*)

* Non-violence (*Ahimsa*): The guiding line from the scriptures is – *Ahimsa Paramo Dharma!*

* Truthful behaviour at all levels (*Sathyam*)

* Abandonment of anger towards oneself and others (*Krodha-thyaga*)

- * Peaceful attitude developed by control over external/sensory organs *(Saanthi)*

- * Aversion to finding fault with others *(Apaisunam)*

- * Compassion to all beings *(Daya bhutheshu)*

- * Distaste for things unfit for pursuit. Control of desire leading to action to acquire or taste them *(Alolupathvam)*

- * Gentleness to others *(Maardhavam)*

- * The development of a sense of modesty *(Hri)*

- * Absence of fickleness and freedom from temptation *(Vishaya Saanidhya achapalam)*

- * Grandeur or ability to stay over insults of ill meaning ones *(Teja)*

- * Forbearance and tolerance towards those who offend *(Kshama)*

- * Firmness of resolve even during times of danger *(Dhruthi);* the ability to think of the Lord with resolve at those times instead of panicking

- * Cleanliness and purity of body, mind and speech *(Soucham)*

- * Freedom from hatred and control of unfair conduct to those weaker than us *(adhroham)*

*   Control over pride and arrogance
    (Naathimanitha)

When we cultivate these attributes, we acquire *daiva sampadi* or Divine heritage.

What can we say about those with demoniacal qualities? The Lord takes great pains to describe these in detail so that men of right thinking can avoid them, even weed them out if they happen to be present in us. Not only are all the above mentioned Divine qualities completely absent in those with aspects of *asuramsam,* but they also exhibit the following traits: they are devoid of purity, good conduct and truth; they lack faith in God or any other Superior Power beyond the material world; they are dull of understanding and cruel in their thoughts and deeds; self-conceited, arrogant, stubborn and greedy, they are slaves to their own insatiable desires, and beset by needless cares and fears, they become their own worst enemies as well as the destroyers of others' happiness. Their lives ultimately end in misery and degradation. Haughtiness, arrogance and egoism lead to this dire fate.

For Your Reflection

The Varaha Purana *tells us that one of the surest means of salvation is singing His glory (Gana Rupa Upayam). This is what we call* kirtan *in our* satsang, *singing the Name of the Lord in praise and prayer. To illustrate this, the Lord narrated the following story to His Consort, Bhoomi Devi.*

Long ago there lived a humble man, a chandaala belonging to a low caste, who was deeply devout, pious and virtuous. Everyone in his village knew him by the name of Nampaduvan (our singer); for it was his daily habit to go to the temple and spend a few hours singing the glory of God. He fasted strictly on Ekadasi *days, and on the night of* Ekadasi, *he would spend the entire night in a vigil, standing and singing outside the temple. At daybreak on the following day, he would return home, have a bath and then break the fast with a traditional* dwadasi paranam.

One Ekadasi *day, as Nampaduvan was hurrying to the temple, he was confronted by a Brahma rakshasa who threatened to devour him as food instantly. Nampaduvan explained to the demon about his* Ekadasi *fast and his vow to keep a singing vigil outside the temple. "Please let me go now so that I may fulfill the obligations of my* vrata," *he begged the demon. "Once I have offered my* kirtan *to the*

Lord, I promise you, I shall come back to offer myself as food to you."

The Brahma rakshasa was mightily impressed by the poor man's sincerity and earnestness, and allowed him to go at once so that he may fulfill his vow and come back to him.

Nampaduvan hurried to the temple and offered his soulful songs to the Lord. As dawn broke, he hurried back to the thickly wooded area where he had met the demon, to keep up his promise to the creature.

The demon was taken aback to see him again. In truth, he had taken pity on the poor man and let him off, not really believing that anyone would ever come back to be devoured by him. "You are a man of truth and integrity," he said to Nampaduvan. "I free you from your promise; you may go."

"But I cannot do that," Nampaduvan insisted. "Today is the sacred dwadasi day, and I must keep up the vow I made to you on Ekadasi. I am indeed blessed that instead of just offering food to a brahmin, I can become food to someone like you."

The Brahma rakshasa was so moved that he began to cry. "I am no ordinary demon," he said to Nampaduvan. "I was a learned brahmin called Somasarma in my previous birth, and was cursed by my elders because I was careless in performing the daily yajnas. *You can help me achieve liberation, if only you agree to give me the* phala *or fruit of your devout* kirtan *before the Lord.*"

"But I cannot do that," Nampduvan explained. "I sing before the Lord in absolute devotion and a spirit of surrender, without any expectation of reward or punya. How can I give away what I do not have?"

"Alas," sighed the brahma rakshasa. "I shall be condemned to live forever as a demon, eating human flesh. When will my misfortune ever come to an end? When can I ever hope to attain to the Lotus Feet of the Lord?"

Nampaduvan was filled with pity for the dejected demon. "I freely and whole heartedly offer you the fruit of the last song that I sang to the Lord this morning," he said to the demon. "If my devotion has the power to move the Lord, may He grant you freedom from the curse laid on you."

No sooner had he spoken, than the demon was transformed into a spirit, and the spirits from the heaven-world came to escort him to the land of the Blessed.

Somasarma was born a Brahmin, *but became a* Rakshasa, *while Nampaduvan, who was born a* Chandala *was able to expiate him of all his sins.*

Therefore we may learn that birth and caste are not a criterion for us to respect anyone. His deep devotion to the Lord, his adherence to the truth and the readiness to renounce worldly pleasures are very important criteria. The caste is physical. It does not belong to the soul. Hence Nampaduvan was elevated to the highest order. Even today, the story of Nampaduvan is narrated and acted out in Vaishnava temples in South India on the sacred day of Kaisika Ekadasi. *It is believed by the devout that listening to this story can expiate them of all their accumulated sins.*

Questions:

1. Can you identify your divine and demoniacal qualities?

2. If, like most people, you too have a mixture of the divine and demoniacal heritage, what will you do to enhance the former and negate the latter?

3. When you first read about or heard of *daivasura sampadi,* what was your first reaction — to evaluate yourself or to judge others whom you know?

4. Fault-finding, according to Gurudev Sadhu Vaswani, is an attribute of the demoniacal. Have you eliminated this quality in you?

Exercises:

The Lord tells us in this chapter that the Divine heritage can lead us to *moksha* or liberation, while the demoniacal qualities will lead us to those triple gates of hell. How can we ensure our liberation against the force of our own negative nature?

According to Hindu philosophy, we believe that we are bound by the law of *karma,* and that our personality, our character and temperament, and even our *swabhava* or nature, are determined by our past *karma.* This will make you wonder whether your own effort or voluntary action has anything to do with your liberation. After all, if everything is *predetermined,* what is the use of human effort?

In one of our ancient texts, the *Yoga Vashishta*, Sri Rama's Guru, sage Vashishta, assures him that self-effort can lead to liberation, and that man has infinite freedom to achieve his liberation through self-effort. Liberation is not determined by destiny; liberation cannot be predicted by astrology or palmistry. Liberation is achieved only through self-effort and the grace of God or the Guru. In this process, you will need the guidance of a Guru, whose moral support can help you on the path. Self-effort is necessary to surrender your will to the Guru, and to pursue the path with faith and devotion.

When you follow the right direction, you will soon realise that you are being drawn towards Divine grace. Your self-effort has led you to this beautiful state, which is the ultimate condition of human life. Many people are often confused about the balance between self-effort and Divine grace. What is the Dividing line between the two? Does self-effort cease when divine grace operates?

Our scriptures distinguish four aspects of divine grace, *Ishwara, Kripa, Guru Kripa, Shastra Kripa* and *Atma Kripa*.

Ishwara Kripa is the Divine assistance that comes to our aid when all else fails us. Consider the plight of Draupadi, as she was about to be disgraced, dishonoured, de-robed by the Kauravas. King Dritarashtra did nothing to stop the dastardly deed of his sons; the Kuru elders, Bhishma, Drona, Kripa were powerless in the face of such evil; as for her five husbands – they bowed down their heads in utter humiliation and shame. All earthly sources of help failed Draupadi utterly, in her hour of desperate, piteous need.

However, Draupadi knew that there was One whose grace is unfailing. One, whose support is perennial. Therefore, she called upon Sri Krishna. He came to her aid promptly.

We have all benefited from *Ishwara Kripa* in our lives, though circumstances might not have been so dramatic. Think of such occasions as this – when you narrowly escaped a fall, or a motor accident; when you miss a train or a flight, and learn later that it met with a crash/disaster. It is God's grace that has saved you, though we acknowledge this only on rare occasions and during momentous events.

Guru Kripa or the grace of the Guru, is the amazing protection that the Guru offers to his disciples. When we surrender ourselves to his will utterly and completely, the Guru's guidance is made available to us at every step.

Shahstra Kripa, the grace of the scriptures is not obtained merely by reading the words or the pages of the sacred texts. It is when you approach the scriptures in the right frame of mind, with the right attitude, and eager to assimilate their truth, that their essential meaning is revealed to you. When you internalise the truth of the texts you read, and not merely quote or recite from them, you have reached a crucial stage in your spiritual development.

Atma Kripa or *Sva Kripa* (the grace of your own soul) enables you to take a deep interest in spiritual matters. You are not distracted by materialistic goals; worldly affairs do not take you away from the chosen path to God; you are not tempted by the passing shadows of life. The grace of the soul enables you to pursue the pilgrim path with patience and perseverance.

All these four aspects represent Divine Grace in different manifestations. We need to be receptive, to benefit from them. Like the quality of Mercy that Shakespeare spoke of, Divine mercy "is not strained"; it too, "droppeth as the gentle rain from heaven". Nowadays, we talk of rain-harvesting, which requires special efforts and specific arrangements. So too, if we are to receive Divine grace, we must learn to become willing receptacles to the same. This is possible through *sadhana* or spiritual discipline.

Sadhana too, is a matter of self-effort. Of course, this effort must not be tainted by egoism, greed or pride. But this becomes possible when we realise the ever-loving presence of God in our lives, and surrender ourselves to His Grace. You realise then, the crucial inter-dependence between your effort and His Grace, which leads to liberation.

Chapter - XVII

Shraddha Traya Vibhaga Yoga

The title of this chapter is translated as "The Yoga of the Threefold Division of Faith". Gurudev Sadhu Vaswani referred to this simply as "Three Kinds of Faith". Some translators call it "The Three Divisions of Material Existence".

Shraddha, as we know, is faith – implicit faith. Sri Krishna tells us how we may apply our faith practically to make our lives lead us Godward.

What happens in this chapter

At the end of Chapter 16, the Lord had stated that anyone who fails to follow the law of the scriptures, but follows instead his own physical desires and willful impulses cannot attain liberation from the perpetual cycle of birth and death.

Arjuna is worried: what of men who are ignorant of the scriptural laws, but live and act with utter devotion to the Lord? What is their condition? What is the nature of their faith?

The Lord now enlightens him on three kinds of faith which are inherent in human nature – *sattvic, rajasic* and *tamasic.*

The *guna* which dominates in us, also determines the kind of faith we develop: if we are *sattvic,* our faith is pure; if *rajas* dominates in us, our faith is clouded by worldly intentions; and if *tamas* is dominant, our faith is selfish, impure and dark.

The *gunas* in turn, are determined by the food we eat, which also determines our activities, such as the kind of sacrifices, austerities and charity that we practise. Those acts performed in the right spirit, with the right faith, lead to liberation; in the absence of true faith, all actions are barren and useless.

There is no need to renounce actions, sacrifices, austerities and charity in order to attain the Lord. All that is required is that we surrender all these actions to Him, we must perform all these activities as worship of God, in the spirit of *arpanam* and surrender, which is done by uttering the *vedic mantra, Om Tat Sat.* This means that all our actions are done for His sake; we do not expect to gain anything from them; all that we wish is for God to accept them. Thus are all our activities purified and sanctified and made acceptable to the Lord.

Om Tat Sat: this is considered to be the threefold designation of Brahman. By this were ordained of old the Brahmins, the Vedas and the sacrifices. [XVII:23]

Om Tat Sat is the Gita's *mantra:* its repetition is a sacramental act which opens the doors of grace to us. It is the *mantra* of faith.

Whatsoever is done without faith, whether it be offering (in sacrifice), gift or austerity, or anything else, is called *asat*. O Arjuna! Such work is of no value hereafter or here. [XVII:28]

Think About it...

Who can comprehend Thee if You do not reveal Thyself, O Lord! *Vedas* and *Vedanta* cannot be the final word on Your Existence. Beings go madly searching, moving in circles in the darkness, performing sacrifices and austerities which are mere activities. But how can actions ever lead to realisation of your true nature!

Creation, preservation and destruction are your modes of *maya*. In them lies no substance whatsoever – they are illusory projections. It is like trying to catch hold of empty space with your hands. Caught in *maya*, circling in cycle rounds, beings act on their desires, but who is it that infuses us with these desires, O Lord!

The impossible becomes easy when you shower your blessings upon us. And it is this alone that causes me to hold to this life and body. O Compassionate One, do shower those blessings upon me. Come and dwell permanently and lovingly in my lotus heart.

— Rabindranath Tagore

For Your Reflection

The Gopis were waiting anxiously on the banks of the River Jamuna. They were filled with the utmost longing to cross the river and go to Mathura to see their beloved Krishna. But the river was in spate, and there was no boatman around to row them across to the other shore.

As luck would have it, Sage Veda Vyasa arrived at the river edge. The Gopis ran to him, offered their humble pranams to him and begged him to help them cross the river.

"First and foremost, you must offer me some food," the sage said to them.

The Gopis brought him plenty of milk and butter, and the sage ate his fill. Now he turned to the river and said: "O, Jamuna, if you believe the truth that I have not eaten anything today, may your waters part and allow us to cross to the other shore in safety."

Immediately, the waters of the Jamuna parted, and the delighted Gopis rushed across to meet their Beloved.

This is a story of food and faith! Veda Vyasa asked for food and got it; but it was his firm conviction that Sriman Narayana, the Supreme Lord, dwelt within him, and that all that he said and did and ate were in fact, prompted and accomplished by the Lord Himself. Thus, if he ate food, that too, was but an offering to the Lord. Though he had eaten his fill of the milk and butter brought to him, he knew that it was the Lord who had taken it. And so when he asserted that he had not eaten anything, the Jamuna took his word for it. It was faith that took the Gopis to Sri Krishna; it was faith that removed all the obstacles on their journey, and faith that parted the waters of the swollen river. It was faith that gave Veda Vyasa the power to call upon the river to oblige him.

Questions:

In this Chapter, Sri Krishna asks us to evaluate our habits, attitude and conduct.

1. What kind of food do we eat?
2. What are the austerities/devotional practices/ kinds of worship that we practise?
3. Do we practise charity/giving? If so, do we give in public or private?
4. What are our real motives in performing worship and in giving?

We would do well to introspect on these motives, in the light of what the Lord tells us in this chapter.

Practical Suggestions:

The Gita's Good Food Guide

Man cannot live without air, water and food. While air and water are available to us in the natural state, food is selected, prepared and eaten by our own choice.

The Gita tells us that food is of three types – *sattvic, rajasic* and *tamasic.*

Sattvic foods contribute to inner calm and peace of mind. They induce pious thoughts and feelings. They keep us in a state of emotional poise and equanimity.

Rajasic foods incite passion and give rise to restlessness.

Tamasic foods induce dullness, inertia and lethargy. They also give rise to impure thoughts.

Sattvic food gives us just the right amount of energy, not too much or too little. But *sattvic* food is easily digestible, leaving us with sufficient energy balance to devote to our work. It is rich in proteins, carbohydrates, vitamins and fibres. *Sattvic* food also calms our senses.

Rajasic foods give us plenty of energy, but we spend much of it in digesting and eliminating such food. As it contains energy-enhancers, there is greater likelihood of toxin build-up in the body, if this energy is not fully utilised. Ayurvedic physicians tell us that rich foods in this category generate stress, causing respirative, renal or cardiac disorders. *Rajasic* food also causes obesity, diabetes and ulcers.

Tamasic food gives very little energy, but is difficult to digest. It also generates a lot of toxins in the system.

The ideal diet is one that avoids *rajasic* and *tamasic* foods. You will not be surprised to know that what the ancient Hindu scriptures regarded as *sattvic* food is now held up to be the ideal food, although by other names! Experts call it high-fibre, natural, anti-oxidant, etc. and we are encouraged to eat more of such foods. As for what the sages called *rajasic, tamasic* food, the very same foods are now labelled high-fat, high-cholestrol, carcinogenic, etc. and we are warned to keep them out of our diets to the greatest extent possible!

In the Gita, Sri Krishna urges Arjuna to adhere to a *sattvic* diet. Such a diet is simple and nutritious;

it gives adequate energy and is easily digested. It is wholesome and non-toxic. It affords immense variety, and is also pleasing to the eye and palate.

Fruits and Vegetables

Fruits have been described as the food of the Gods, and also the food of the *rishis* and *yogis*. They are nature's own special delicacies, brought to luscious goodness in the warmth of the sun. They are rich in vitamins and minerals, and also give us plenty of fibre. For example, oranges, grape-fruits and lemons are the best source of vitamin C. They are also rich in a readily digestible form of sugar which gives us instant energy without the harmful effects of refined sugar.

Cooking destroys vital vitamins in fruits. The same is true of dried fruits, which retain their energy, but lose much of their nutritive value. Tinned fruits are best avoided – for they contain preservatives that are poisonous. For all these reasons, it is best to eat fresh, ripe fruits in season.

We in India are lucky to have a choice of such a wide variety of fruits throughout the year, green and black grapes, strawberries from the hills, delicious watermelons and musk melons, mango – the King of fruits, pears, apples, peaches, lichees, papayas, pomegranates, guavas, chikkus, berries – and at least a hundred varieties of banana!

The most expensive fruits are not the most nutritious either! The old-fashioned proverb may tell us, an apple a day keeps the doctor away. But the poor man's fruit, banana, contains far more nutrition and goodness than an expensive apple!

Vegetables are Mother Nature's marvellous products. Her Divine garden truly presents a blaze of brilliant colours with the red and yellow, green and purple, pink, white, brown and mauve of these delicious wonders!

A vegetarian connoisseur will be proud to tell you that you can effortlessly put together a balanced diet just by choosing a bit of each colour!

Vegetables are not only a treat to the eye, they cater to all tastes and palates. Green leafy vegetables, tubors like potatoes, yam and beetroot, soft vegetables like zucchini and pumpkin, as well as popular treats like cabbage, cauliflowers, beans, aubergines, tomatoes, garlic, peas, onions – not to mention delicious herbs like coriander, basil, parsley, etc.

A balanced mix of leafy vegetables, 'seed' vegetables and pulses produces a perfect combination in terms of nutrition and energy. Salads are surely everyone's favourite!

A Vegetarian Diet

In practical terms food can be of two categories: food of violence or *himsa,* food that includes fish, flesh and fowl; the alternative is the food of *ahimsa* or non-violence, in other words, a vegetarian diet.

During the last fifty years or more, medical experts and nutritionists have largely inclined to the opinion that a vegetarian diet is the best option for good health.

Anatomical and physiological studies point to the fact that a civilised, evolved man is meant to be a vegetarian. His entire digestive system, including his teeth, his stomach and his intestines are so structured as to prove that even nature meant him to be a vegetarian.

A vegetarian diet includes all of the following, - grains such as rice, wheat, maize, millets, etc; pulses such as dals and lentils, roots and tubors like potatoes, carrots and onions; fresh and dry fruits, like apples, mango, water-melon, banana, as well as almonds, cashews, peanuts, etc; and the abundant and plentiful supply of fresh, green, leafy and non-leafy vegetables that God has blessed the earth with!

There are some people who claim that milk is an animal product and therefore should not be included in a strictly vegetarian diet. But the fact remains, that we do not kill a cow to obtain its milk.

Mahatma Gandhi who was an ardent advocate of a vegan diet, one which did not include milk, excluded milk totally from his diet for about six years or so. Then in 1917, he fell ill, and in his own words, "was reduced to a skeleton". The doctors warned him that he would not be able to build up enough strength to leave his bed, if milk and milk products were not included in his diet. However, Gandhiji had made a vow that he would not take milk. A doctor then suggested to him that when he had made the vow, he could only have had in mind the milk of the cow and the buffalo, so the vow should not prevent him from taking goat's milk! That was how Gandhiji began to take goat's milk. At that time, he himself admitted, it seemed to bring him new life! He picked up rapidly and was soon able to leave his sickbed. "On account of this and several similar experiences," he writes, "I have been forced to admit the necessity of adding milk to the strict vegetarian diet."

At that time, Gandhiji wrote prophetically: "I am convinced that in the vast vegetable kingdom there must be some kind, which, while supplying those necessary substances which we derive from milk, is free from its ethical drawbacks."

Nutrition experts now feel that soya milk and tofu can indeed provide such an alternative.

Here are a few simple suggestions you can follow in your diet:

1. Offer a simple prayer of gratitude to the Lord before you eat your food. Remember, that food that is eaten as *prasadam,* purifies you.

2. Do not drink water along with your meals. Water dilutes the digestive juices and this may retard digestion.

3. Rest for half an hour or so after you eat i.e. refrain from physical labour. The energy of the body must not be diverted from the main job of digestion.

4. All the food that you eat must be chewed thoroughly: for the process of digestion begins in the mouth. Mastication – chewing – aids the digestion process.

5. Try to avoid eating between meals: snacking is not a healthy habit and only overburdens the digestive tract.

6. Wash and peel fruits and vegetables. We live in an age when organically grown products are rare. The poisonous residues from chemical sprays and insecticides may cling to the surface of the fruits/ vegetables. Washing and peeling are therefore very essential.

7. Most important of all, eat at fixed times. Eat only when you are hungry. Do not eat by the clock. If you have no appetite, you will do well to skip a meal occasionally.

8. Drink plenty of water during the day. Coffee, tea and soft drinks are best avoided. Experts remark that all liquid apart from water is "either a food or a poison."

Chapter - XVIII

Moksha Sannyasa Yoga

Gurudev Sadhu Vaswani translated this title as "The Yoga Of Liberation Through Renunciation". In this chapter, he said, is given to us, "The Final Word" of the Lord on the subject of liberation. Thus, some scholars refer to this chapter as "The Final Revelation of the Ultimate Truth".

We have been attending a heavenly symphony of grace and wisdom, listening to the Song Divine of Sri Krishna. Now, finally, the various strands of the magnificent symphony are brought together in the One ultimate message that is the Lord's sacred promise to all of us: Come to Me for thy salvation.

What happens in this chapter

The conclusion of the song supreme, encapsulates the whole message of the Gita. In a brief, masterly summary, the Divine teacher ensures that his dear, devoted disciple achieves self-mastery and enlightenment.

The ultimate message of the Gita is this: by doing our *swadharma,* we can attain liberation. The only requisite is that we should surrender all our actions to the Lord, and give up attachment, egoism, selfishness and desire. When we offer our duty as worship of God, we obtain His Grace and attain to Him.

Sri Krishna gives us his special interpretation of the two key words in the Gita, namely *Sannyasa* and *Tyaga.* Performing our duties without worldly objectives, without expectation of rewards is *sannyasa.* Sacrificing the fruits of our action is *tyaga.* The duty allotted to us in this life constitutes our *swadharma;* performing one's own *dharma* (even if it may be with our deficiencies and mistakes) is far better than performing the *dharma* of others, at its best.

The Lord has already spoken to Arjuna in

great detail about *karma yoga, gnana yoga* and *bhakti yoga.* Now, He gives Arjuna the freedom to choose the option that he wishes to choose. And, to prepare him for the right choice, Sri Krishna also offers him the chance to free himself from the fear of sin, evil, bondage and rebirth into *samsara.* All that Arjuna or, for that matter, any one of us – needs to do is to surrender ourselves to the Lord, absolutely, unconditionally and without any reservations or fear or doubt. This is the beautiful *saranagati tattva* pronounced by the Lord Himself.

Saranagati would clear us of all our sins and pave the way of *bhakti yoga* which will lead us to Sri Krishna. The Lord reiterates His promise to us again and again: He assures us that each and every one of His devotees who has faith in Him and absolutely surrenders to Him (and Him alone) will have nothing to worry as they will surely reach Him at the end of this life.

The Gita is essentially a call to action, this is why Sri Krishna urges us not to renounce action, but to renounce its fruits and attachment to results instead. This, the Lord tells us, is called *tyaga* or sacrifice, by the wise. This is the ideal of *nishkama karma* (desireless action).

Arjuna, at the beginning of the discourse, had failed to understand this ideal as a warrior; he was unwilling to do his duty, because he found it disagreeable and unpleasant to kill his own kinsmen. This was, of course, ignorance. Now, he is enlightened, and exclaims joyfully:

Destroyed is my delusion. I have gained recognition through Thy Grace, O Krishna! I am firm, my doubts have fled. I shall act according to Thy word.

[XVIII:73]

Arjuna is resolved to act now, in full, firm faith and devotion. So can we all, for the Lord's assurance is for all of us too.

Abandoning all duties, come unto Me alone for shelter. Grieve not! I shall liberate thee from all sins. Of this, have no doubt. [XVIII:66]

Think About it...

The Lord's final words in His Divine discourse to Arjuna constitute a brief and practical summing up of all that He has said until now. The teacher beyond compare as He is, He gives us in brief, through selected, important points, all the vital truths He has revealed to us earlier.

We also see here, the effect of the Lord's discourse on Arjuna. The Gita began with Arjuna's utter despondency and despair; it is finally resolved in his triumphant self-mastery, strength and firm determination. The central message of the Gita comes through, clear as crystal: through the performance of one's duties in life, one can qualify for the highest liberation, if one performs all actions by renouncing egoism and attachment and surrendering all desire for selfish, personal gain. By regarding the performance of our duties as worship offered to God, we obtain the Grace of the Lord and attain to His Lotus Feet, the Home that we all came from, and the Home to which we must return. The Divine injunction is that God must be made the sole object, goal and aim of one's life. This injunction is the heart of the Gita. This is the one way to achieve *moksha* or liberation.

For Your Reflection

The Lord is referred to as Deenabandhu *(the friend of the weak and helpless);* Karunasagara *(the ocean of compassion);* Aapatbandhava *and* Anaadarakshaka *(the Protector of those in danger and those without support). He never, ever fails to protect those who surrender to His mercy.*

Many are the inspiring stories told to us in Srimad Bhagavat *on this aspect of the Lord's assurance to us; the stories of Dhruva, Prahlada and Kuchela have become immortal among the devout.*

Equally inspiring is Gajendra Moksham, the deeply symbolic story of the elephant who called upon the Lord for His grace, and was instantly granted freedom from the deadly grip of the crocodile in whose jaws his foot was trapped. It is one of the most famous leelas *of Lord Vishnu in* Srimad Bhagavat. *The devout ones believe that a recitation of this episode early in the morning has the same effect as the recitation of the sacred* Vishnu Sahasranama. *We are assured by sages that there is no disaster from which the compassionate Lord would not protect His dear devotees, who, with faith and devotion remember His Feet as their sole refuge.*

A great and mighty elephant was roaming in

the forest with his females and cubs in tow, when he was overcome by thirst. Parched with thirst, he smelt from afar, the pollen dust of the lotus flower. Rightly surmising that a lake was at hand, he led his troupe in that direction and was delighted to see a huge tank of crystal clear water. The herd stepped into the tank and the tusker splashed water on its young, and felt happy to see his females and cubs refresh themselves by drinking the nectar-like water of the tank.

All of a sudden, disaster struck the leader of the elephants. A powerful crocodile in the waters of the tank suddenly gripped the elephant's foot; caught unawares, the huge tusker found that he was unable to pull himself free from the jaws of the crocodile. The females and cubs were terrified to hear the roar of their leader, and desperately tried to save him, pushing and pulling him from the sides and the rear; but it was to no avail.

The leader was in great pain; and the herd was deeply distressed to see him entrapped and trumpeted in sorrow.

It seemed to go on and on for ever; it was as if the elephant's plight had lasted to eternity. With all his might and power, the enormous tusker just could not pull himself free.

All of a sudden, the realisation dawned on the

elephant that his strength and his power had not prevented him from being caught in the crocodile's jaws: it was God's Will that he should be so entrapped; and it would be God's Will too, that could rescue him from this plight. When this awareness came to him, he gave up the physical struggle to extricate himself, and surrendered himself to the Lord. "Those of my ilk cannot save me," he thought to himself. "How can the females and little ones help? I am caught by the noose of Providence in the shape of the crocodile; therefore, I shall seek Him as my ultimate refuge. I seek the Lotus Feet of the Lord who protects the fearful and helpless creatures of this earth; I seek His refuge, from the powerful jaws of Death that grasp us ever so swiftly, for even Death runs away in utter fear of the Lord."

At this point, the Srimad Bhagavat gives us the hymn to the Lord uttered by the Elephant, who, at the point of immanent death, remembered the hymn that he had uttered in his previous birth. Given below are the opening words of this magnificent hymn to the Lord:

Salutation to that Lord from whom everything sentient arises. To the *Purusha*, the primordial seed, the Lord of all, I bow. I take shelter in Him, in Whom is the entire universe, from Whom it all emanates. Who is Himself its cause and Who is beyond all the utmost beyond...

The Lord rushed to the aid of His devotee, and with His Chakrayuda, cut the crocodile in two, granting both the predator and the victim the liberation that they had sought.

Truly has it been said, that the Lord is Saranagatha Vatsalah; He is ever affectionate towards those who seek refuge in Him.

To those of you who have read the earlier chapters and have now come to share with me the final words of the Lord, the symbolic significance of this story will not be lost. This story is a parable of mankind. Gajendra is everyman. The tank is nothing but the samsara sagara in which all of us are adrift. The herd stands for the kith and kin, family and friends by whom we are surrounded and on whom we tend to rely for all help and support. The crocodile symbolises death and the insurmountable obstacles that come in the way of our ultimate liberation.

None can liberate us from this doomed struggle except the Lord. He is the strength of the week, the support of those who are helpless. He is our ultimate refuge.

Questions:

1. Do you consider yourself a true *bhakta* of the Lord?

2. What is your greatest strength as a devotee?

3. What is your greatest weakness as a devotee?

4. What are the things you want from the Lord?

5. Whom would you call upon in an emergency – your friend, your spouse or your parents?

6. What do you rely on in an emergency – money, power, authority, connections, your own intelligence and resources – or Your Faith?

Practical Suggestions

At the end of His Divine discourse, it is obvious that the Lord recommends *Bhakti Yoga* as the easiest and simplest way to reach Him.

Bhakti Yoga is the path of utter devotion, supreme love for God. It is pure and selfless love, which is far above worldly love. It does not involve bargaining with God over results; it is above all selfish motives. It is intense devotion and attachment to the Lord. It has to be felt, experienced, not talked about or discussed.

* *Bhakti* pervades the devotee's heart, mind and soul.

* In its intensity, all impurities of the mind are destroyed, reduced to ashes.

* It makes the devotee simple and childlike in his absolute trust in God.

*   It has none of the weaknesses and defects of human love – like selfishness, insincerity, attachment and ego.

*   It is the most pure and natural form of love, for we learn to love God even as He loves us.

What are the qualities of a true *bhakta*?

*   He has a soft, loving, tender heart.

*   He is free from pride, lust and anger, greed and egoism.

*   In his great love for the Lord, he strives for perfection – and ceaselessly works to overcome his defects.

*   He is free from all cares, fears and worries. Like a child, he feels himself safe and secure in the Lord's Divine protection.

*   He treats everybody alike; he does not see people as 'enemies' or 'friends'; all people are his brothers and sisters. His love extends to all alike, for in each and every human being, he perceives the form of the Lord.

*   His faith in the Lord is firm, unwavering and absolute. His strength and courage are derived from this faith. This faith roots out all anxiety and fear from his mind.

*   He is firm in the conviction that all that happens to him, happens for the best, for it

comes as God's Will. Happiness and sorrow are also forms of God's Grace.

Bhakti too requires heroism. In its highest stages, the devotee even refrains from asking God to take away his pain, misery and suffering. Thus, it was that Kunti Devi prayed to Sri Krishna: "O Lord, let me always have adversity, so that my mind may be ever fixed at Thy Feet."

Yes, pain and suffering are to be welcomed, accepted, for they help us remember God constantly. They are blessings in disguise, for they help to free us from the bondage of this world. When we go through adversity, God also bestows upon us the wisdom, courage endurance and spiritual strength to overcome this adversity. In fact, the Lord puts His devotees through severe tests and trials only in order that they may be moulded, purified, evolved and made fit to receive His divine vision. Does He not tell us in the Gita:

Yet not by the Vedas, nor by austerities, nor by gifts, nor by sacrifices, can I be seen in the Form in which thou (Arjuna) dost see Me.

But by devotion to Me alone, devotion undivided – may I thus be known and seen in essence, and entered into, O Arjuna! [XI:53:54]

What is the best way to develop such love for the Lord? The answer is simple: we begin with *Guru bhakti.*

The Guru gives us a form, a visible outer form which we can take to represent God. To serve and worship the Guru is the best way to cultivate devotion for the Lord.

Beginning with ordinary *bhakti,* which for most of us is worship of a form or an idol, eventually leads to *para bhakti,* the highest form of devotion in which the devotee feels completely one with the Lord. He sees the Lord in all, he sees everything, everyone as the Lord's manifestation.

Para bhakti eventually leads to *gnana,* the highest wisdom. Both *gnana* and *para bhakti* enable us to attain liberation, union with the Lord – which is the goal of all *sadhana* and *abhaysa.*

Let us learn to rely more and more on God. God invites us to surrender ourselves to Him, and offer all our efforts to Him in the spirit of dedication – as Krishna *Arpanam.* He invites us to hand our problems over to Him.

Do you have a better option than the best?

The Final Message

The Lord's teachings comes to an end with *Sloka* 71, Chapter XVIII. The marvellous Master that He is, the Lord asks Arjuna:

> Has this been heard by you, O Arjuna, with one-pointed mind? Has thy *moha* (delusion) caused by *agnana* (ignorance) been destroyed?   [XVIII: 72]

What follows are the final verses spoken by Arjuna and Sanjaya in the Mahabharata. They form a fitting conclusion to the Divine Discourse which we were privileged to hear through the grace of the Lord, Guru Veda Vyasa and his devout disciple, Sanjaya.

Arjuna said:

Destroyed is my delusion. I have gained recognition through Thy Grace, O Krishna! I am firm, my doubts have fled. I shall act according to Thy Word.

Arjuna's doubts are now at an end. His mind stands firm. Light has come to him; *smriti,* recognition has dawned upon him. He has learnt the true nature of the *Atman,* of the knowledge of essential Truth. The veil of illusion has been torn asunder from his eyes. He realises that as a *jivatma,* his highest wisdom is to surrender to the Divine Spirit. He says: "I will obey."

So it should be with us all. When the *jiva* realises its true nature, egoism is destroyed. Illusions disappear. Doubts are dispelled. We hear the voice of God within – the still, small voice, and we begin to act, as instruments of the Lord.

Sanjaya said:

Thus, have I heard this marvellous dialogue between Vasudeva and the great-souled Partha, causing my hair to stand on end.

By the grace of Vyasa I heard this supreme secret, this *yoga* taught by Krishna himself, the Lord of *yoga,* speaking before me.

All along, it is through Sanjaya's narrative to Dhritarashtra that the Bhagavad Gita has been reported to us. Sanjaya has also been privileged to see that ecstatic vision of the Lord's *Viswarupa Darshana* that Arjuna beheld – with the special perception granted to him by Ved Vyasa.

> Remembering, remembering this marvellous and holy dialogue between Krishna and Arjuna, O King, I thrill with joy, again and again!

> Remembering, remembering also that most marvellous form of Krishna, great is my wonder, O King, and I thrill with joy, again and again!

Never before has such a conversation ever taken place, between a struggling, seeking *jivatma* and the Mighty Lord Himself, the *Paramatma.* Sanjaya has heard it, and thanks to his narration, we have been blessed to hear it too, as it happened.

Let us not forget, Vyasa was the spiritual master of Sanjaya, and it is the master's grace that made it possible for Sanjaya to be part of this illuminating discourse. By the grace of Vyasa, his senses were purified, and he could see and hear Sri Krishna directly.

The Gita's message is crystal clear: the essence of faith, the ultimate goal of what we call religion, *(dharma)* is to surrender ourselves at the Lord's Feet absolutely and unconditionally. This is the highest perfection that human beings are capable of. The way of *gnana,* or philosophical speculation and *dhyana,* meditation are not accessible to us all. But the way of devotion and loving surrender, the *bhakti marga* is open to the least amongst us.

> *Yatra Yogesvarah Krsno*
> *Yatra Partho Dhanur-Dharah*
> *Tatra Srir Vijayo Bhutir*
> *Dhruva Nitir Matir Mama*

Wherever there is Krishna, the Lord of *Yoga,* wherever is Arjuna, the archer, assured are there prosperity, victory, welfare and *neeti* (righteousness or morality).

Appendix - 1

Gita Mahatmya — The Glory of the Gita

(From the Varaha Purana)

Many are the sages and saints who have composed songs and *slokas* commemorating the greatness of the Gita. Given below is the *Gita Mahatmya* from the *Varaha Purana*, in which Lord Vishnu outlines the glory of the Gita to Mother Earth:

Dharovaacha:

Bhagavan Parameshaana Bhaktiravyabhichaarinee;
Praarabdham Bhujyamaanasya Katham Bhavati
He Prabho.

The Earth said:

1. O *Bhagavan,* the Supreme Lord! How can unflinching devotion arise in him who is immersed in his *Prarabdha Karmas* (worldly life), O Lord?

Sri Vishnuruvaacha:

Praarabdham Bhujyamaano Hi Geetaabhyaasaratah Sadaa;
Sa Muktah Sa Sukhee Loke Karmanaa Nopalipyate.

Lord Vishnu said:

2. Though engaged in the performance of worldly duties, one who is regular in the study of the Gita becomes free. He is a happy man in this world. He is not bound by *karma.*

Mahaapaapaadipaapaani Geetaadhyaanam Karoti Chet;
Kwachit Sparsham Na Kurvanti Nalineedalam Ambuvat.

3. Just as the water stains not the lotus leaf, even so sins do not taint him who is regular in the reading of the Gita.

Geetaayaah Pustakam Yatra Yatra Paathah Pravartate;
Tatra Sarvaani Teerthaani Prayaagaadeeni Tatra Vai.

4. All the sacred centres of pilgrimage, like Prayag and other places, dwell in that place where the Gita is kept, and where the Gita is read.

Sarve Devaashcha Rishayo Yoginahpannagaashcha Ye;
Gopaalaa Gopikaa Vaapi Naaradoddhava Paarshadaih.

5. All the gods, sages, *yogins,* divine serpents, *gopalas, gopikas* (friends and devotees of Lord Krishna), Narada, Uddhava and others dwell here.

Sahaayo Jaayate Sheeghram Yatra Geetaa Pravartate;
Yatra Geetaavichaarashcha Pathanam Paathanam Shrutam;

Tatraaham Nishchitam Prithvi Nivasaami Sadaiva Hi.

6. Help comes quickly where the Gita is recited and, O Earth, I ever dwell where it is read, heard, taught and contemplated upon!

Geetaashraye'ham Tishthaami Geetaa Me Chottamam Griham;
Geetaajnaanam Upaashritya Treen Uokaan Paalayaamyaham.

7. I take refuge in the Gita, and the Gita is my best abode. I protect the three worlds with the knowledge of the Gita.

Geetaa me paramaa vidyaa brahmaroopaa na samshayah;
Ardhamaatraaksharaa nityaa swaanirvaachyapadaatmikaa.

8. The Gita is my highest science, which is doubtless of the form of Brahman, the Eternal, the *Ardhamaatra* (of the *Pranava* Om), the ineffable splendour of the Self.

Chidaanandena Krishnena Proktaa Swamukhato'rjuna;
Vedatrayee Paraanandaa Tatwaarthajnaanasamyutaa.

9. It was spoken by the blessed Lord Krishna, the all-knowing, through His own mouth, to Arjuna. It contains the essence of the Vedas, the knowledge of the Reality. It is full of supreme bliss.

Yoashtaadasha Japen Nityam Naro Nishchalamaanasah;
Jnaanasiddhim Sa Labhate Tato Yaati Param Padam.

10. He who recites the eighteen chapters of the Bhagavad Gita daily, with a pure and unshaken mind, attains perfection in knowledge, and reaches the highest state or supreme goal.

Paathe'asamarthah Sampoornam Tato'rdham Paathamaacharet;
Tadaa Godaanajam Punyam Labhate Naatra Samshayah.

11. If a complete reading is not possible, even if only half is read, he attains the benefit of giving a cow as a gift. There is no doubt about this.

Tribhaagam Pathamaanastu Gangaasnaanaphalam Labhet;
Shadamsham Japamaanastu Somayaagaphalam Labhet.

12. He who recites one-third part of it achieves the merit of a bath in the sacred river Ganges; and who recites one-sixth of it attains the merit of performing a *Soma* sacrifice (a kind of ritual).

Ekaadhyaayam Tu Yo Nityam Pathate Bhaktisamyutah;
Rudralokam Avaapnoti Gano Bhootwaa Vasecchiram.

13. That person who reads one discourse with supreme faith and devotion attains to the world of *Rudra* and, having become a *Gana* (an attendant of Lord Shiva), lives there for many years.

Adhyaayam Shlokapaadam Vaa Nityam Yah Pathate Narah;
Sa Yaati Narataam Yaavanmanwantaram Vasundhare.

14. If one reads a discourse or even a part of a verse daily he, O Earth, one retains a human body till the end of a *Manvantara,*

Geetaayaah Shloka Dashakam Sapta Pancha Chatushtayam;
Dwautreenekam Tadardhamvaa Shlokaanaam Yah Pathennarah.
Chandralokam Avaapnoti Varshaanaam Ayutam Dhruvam;
Geetaapaathasamaayukto Mrito Maanushataam Vrajet.

15.-16. He who repeats ten, seven, five, four, three, two verses or even one or half of it, attains the region of the moon and lives there for 10,000 years. Accustomed to the daily study of the Gita, a dying man comes back to life again as a human being.

Geetaabhyaasam Punah Kritwaa Labhate Muktim Uttamaam;
Geetetyucchaarasamyukto Mriyamaano Gatim Labhet.

17. By repeated study of the Gita, he attains liberation. Uttering the word Gita at the time of death, a person attains liberation.

Geetaarthashravanaasakto Mahaapaapayuto'pi Vaa;
Vaikuntham Samavaapnoti Vishnunaa Saha Modate.

18. Though full of sins, one who is ever intent on hearing the meaning of the Gita, goes to the Kingdom of God and rejoices with Lord Vishnu.

Geetaartham Dhyaayate Nityam Kritwaa Karmaani Bhoorishah;
Jeevanmuktah Sa Vijneyo Dehaante Paramam

Padam.

19. He who meditates on the meaning of the Gita, having performed many virtuous actions, attains the supreme goal after death. Such an individual should be considered a true *Jivanmukta*.

Geetaam Aashritya Bahavo Bhoobhujo Janakaadayah;
Nirdhootakalmashaa Loke Geetaa Yaataah Param Padam.

20. In this world, taking refuge in the Gita, many Kings like Janaka and others reached the highest state or goal, purified of all sins.

Geetaayaah Pathanam Kritwaa Maahaatmyam Naiva Yah Pathet;
Vrithaa Paatho Bhavet Tasya Shrama Eva Hyudaahritah.

21. He who fails to read this "Glory of the Gita" after having read the Gita, loses the benefit thereby, and the effort alone remains.

Etanmaahaatmyasamyuktam Geetaabhyaasam Karoti Yah;
Sa Tatphalamavaapnoti Durlabhaam Gatim Aapnuyaat.

22. One who studies the Gita, together with this "Glory of the Gita", attains the fruits mentioned above, and reaches the state which is otherwise very difficult to be attained.

Suta Uvaacha:

Maahaatmyam Etad Geetaayaah Mayaa Proktam Sanaatanam;
Geetaante Cha Pathedyastu Yaduktam Tatphalam Labhet.

Suta said:

23. This greatness or "Glory of the Gita", which is eternal, as narrated by me, should be read at the end of the study of the Gita, and the fruits mentioned therein will be obtained.

Iti Srivaraahapuraane Srigeetaamaahaatmyam Sampoornam.

Thus ends the "Glory of the Gita" contained in the Varaha Purana.

Appendix - 2

THE
BHAGAVAD GITA

(Abridged)

The Bhagavad Gita consists of 701 slokas. Of them I have selected 205 slokas which could easily be recited everyday and which, to my mind, give us the essence of the teaching, which the Lord (Sri Krishna) gave to His dear, devoted disciple, Arjuna, on the battle-field of Kurukshetra.

Arjuna saw standing there (on the opposite camp) uncles and grandfathers, teachers, mother's brothers, sons and grandsons, cousins and comrades.   [I:26]

Arjuna was deeply moved to pity and uttered this in sadness.
Seeing these, my kinsmen, O Krishna, arrayed and eager for fight. [I:28]

My limbs fail and my mouth is parched, my body quivers and my hair stands on end. [I:29]

If the sons of Dhritarashtra, weapons in hand, should slay me, while I remain unresisting and unarmed, that would for me be better. [I:46]

Having spoken thus, on the battlefield, Arjuna sank down on his chariot-seat, casting away his bow and arrow, his mind overwhelmed by grief. [I:47]

To Arjuna, thus with pity overcome, with eyes dimmed with tears, despondent, Krishna spoke these words:
[II:1]

The Blessed Lord said:

Yield not to unmanliness. O Arjuna! It doth not befit thee. Cast off the impotence of the heart. Arise, O Arjuna! [II:3]

Arjuna said:

How, O Krishna, shall I attack Bhishma and Drona with arrows in battle? Are they not worthy of reverence, O Krishna? [II:4]

Better to live in this world by begging than to slay these noble Gurus (teachers). Slaying them, I should but taste of delights besmeared with blood! [II:5]

Sanjaya said:

Having thus spoken to Krishna, Arjuna said to Him: "I will not fight." And with these words Arjuna fell silent. [II:9]

Then to Arjuna, who remained sorrowing thus in the midst of the two armies, Krishna, smiling as it were, spake the following words. [II:10]

He never is born, nor does he, at any time, die. Nor, having once come to be, does he cease to be. He is unborn, perpetual, eternal, ancient. He is not slain when the body is slain. [II:20]

As a man casts off worn-out garments and puts on others that are new, even so does the embodied soul cast off worn-out bodies and wears others that are new. [II:22]

Weapons cleave him not, nor fire burneth him. Waters wet him not, nor wind drieth him away. [II:23]

If thou art killed, thou wilt win heaven. If thou art victorious, thou wilt enjoy the earth. Therefore, arise, O Son of Kunti (Arjuna), and brace thine arms for battle. [II:37]

Taking alike pleasure and pain, gain and loss, victory and defeat, gird thee for battle. For so thou shalt not sin. [II:38]

Arjuna said:

What is the description of him who (takes alike pleasure and pain, victory and defeat), who has this steady *prajna* (wisdom), who is steadfast in *samadhi* (holy contemplation), absorbed in Brahman, O Krishna? How does he, the man of concentrated, illumined consciousness, speak? How does he sit? How does he walk? [II:54]

The Blessed Lord said:

When a man puts away, O Arjuna, all the desires of his mind and is satisfied in the Self by the Self, then is he called *sthita-prajna*, the steady seer of wisdom. [II:55]

He whose mind is free from anxiety amid pains, indifferent amid pleasures, loosed from passion, fear and rage, he is called a seer illumined. [II:56]

He who, on every side, is without attachment, who neither likes nor dislikes, whatever hap of fair or foul, such an one has understanding established in wisdom. [II:57]

He who withdraws his senses from the objects of sense on every side, as a tortoise draws in his limbs (into a shell), his understanding is firmly set (in wisdom). [II:58]

The objects of sense turn away from the embodied soul who abstains from feeding on them, but relish for them remains. Even relish turneth away from him when the Supreme is seen. [II:59]

O Arjuna! the excited senses impetuously carry away the mind of even a wise man striving after perfection. [II:60]

Having brought all (his senses) under control, he should sit harmonised, I his supreme goal. For he, whose senses are mastered, his understanding is firmly set. [II:61]

When a man dwells in his mind on the objects of sense, he conceives an attachment to them. From attachment ariseth desire. From desire anger cometh forth. [II:62]

From anger arises bewilderment; from bewilderment, loss of memory; from loss of memory, the destruction of understanding (buddhi); from destruction of buddhi, he perishes. [II:63]

But a man of disciplined mind, who moves among sense-objects, with the senses under control and free from attachment and aversion, he goeth to prasadum, peace. [II:64]

For the uncontrolled, there is no buddhi (understanding); nor for the uncontrolled is there concentration. For him without concentration, there is no peace: and for the unpeaceful, how can there be happiness? [II:66]

When the mind runs after the moving senses, it carries away *prajna* (wisdom, understanding), even as the gale carries away a ship on the waters. [II:67]

Therefore, O Arjuna, he whose senses are all withdrawn from the objects of sense, his *buddhi* is firmly set. [II:68]

What is night for all beings is, for the disciplined soul, the time of waking. What is the time of waking for all beings is night for the *muni*, the sage of vision. [II:69]

He into whom all desires flow as rivers flow into the sea, which, though ever being filled, is ever motionless, he attaineth peace, not he who hugs his desires. [II:70]

He who forsaketh all desires and acts free from longing and is selfless and without egoism, he goeth to peace. [II:71]

This is the divine state (*brahmisthiti*), O Arjura! Having attained thereto, none is ever bewildered. Who so even at the end (the hour of death), is established in that state, he goeth to the *brahma-nirvana*, the bliss of God. [II:72]

There are two paths – the path of knowledge (*Gnana Yoga*) and the path of works (*Karma Yoga*). Arjuna asks: Tell me distinctly the one thing by which I can attain to the highest good.

The Blessed Lord said:

Therefore, without attachment, perform always the action which is thy duty, for by doing work without attachment, man verily reacheth the *Parama*, the Supreme. [III:19]

Janaka and others, indeed, attained to perfection by action. And thou, too, shouldst perform action with a view to the welfare of the world. [III:20]

Surrendering all actions unto Me, with thy thoughts resting on the Self supreme, from desire and egoism freed, and of (mental) fever cured, fight thou, O Arjuna! [III:30]

Better is one's own duty (or path or law, *swadharma*), though imperfectly done, than the duty (or law) of another well discharged. Better death in (the discharge of) one's own duty. To follow another's duty is full of danger. [III:35]

The senses, they say, are great. Greater than the senses is the mind. Greater than the mind is the *buddhi* (understanding or rational will). But what is greater than the *buddhi* is He (the *Atman*, the Self). [III:42]

Thus knowing Him (the Self) as greater than the *buddhi*, steadying the (lower) self by the Self, slay, O Arjuna, the enemy in the form of desire, so difficult to overcome. [III:43]

Many births have been left behind by Me and by thee, O Arjuna! I know them all, but thou knowest not thine. [IV:5]

269

Whenever there is decay of *dharma* (righteousness),
O Arjuna, and there is exaltation of *adharma*
(unrighteousness), then I project Myself.   [IV:7]

For the protection of the good, for the destruction of
the wicked, for the sake of establishing righteousness,
I come into birth from age to age.   [IV:8]

However men approach Me, even so do I greet them,
for the path men take from every side is Mine. O
Arjuna!   [IV:11]

Whose works are all free from the moulding of desire
(*kama sankalpa*), whose actions are burnt clean in the
fire of wisdom (*gnana-agni*), him the wise have called
a *pandit* (a man of true learning, a sage).   [IV:19]

Having abandoned attachment to the fruit of action,
ever content, without dependence, he does nothing,
though ever engaged in work.   [IV:20]

Content with whatever comes by chance, free from
the pairs of opposites (*dvandas*), without jealousy,
balanced in success and failure, even when he acts,
he is not bound.   [IV:22]

Of him whose attachments are dead, who is liberated
(*mukta*), whose mind is firmly established in wisdom,
who does work as a sacrifice, of such a man all action
melts away.   [IV:23]

Better than any material sacrifice is *gnana yagna*, the
sacrifice of wisdom, O Arjuna! For all actions, without
any exception, culminate in *gnana* or wisdom. [IV:33]

Learn wisdom thou by humble reverence, by inquiry (investigation) and by service. The wise, the seers of Truth, will instruct thee in wisdom. [IV:34]

Even if thou art the most sinful of all sinners, thou shalt cross over all sin by the raft of wisdom alone. [IV:36]

As the burning fire turns its fuel to ashes, O Arjuna, so doth the fire of wisdom turn to ashes all action. [IV:37]

He who hath renounced action by *yoga* (i.e., by forsaking all reward), who hath by wisdom cut the bonds of doubt, who ever possesses the *Atman* (is ruled by the *Atman*, the Self), actions do not bind him, O Arjuna! [IV:41]

Arjuna said:

Renunciation of action (*karma sanyasa*) Thou praisest, O Krishna, and also the right performance of action (*karma yoga*). Of the two which one is the better? That tell me for certain. [V:1]

The Blessed Lord said:

Sanyasa (renunciation of action) and *karma-yoga* (unselfish performance of action) both lead to supreme bliss. Of the two, *karma-yoga* is, verily, better than *sanyasa*. [V:2]

Who neither hateth nor desireth should be known

as a perpetual *sanyasi*. For, free from *dvandas* (pairs of opposites), he is easily set free from bondage, O Arjuna! [V:3]

He who is devoted to the path of action and is pure in soul, who is master of his self and has conquered the senses, who realises his Self as the Self in all beings, though acting, he is not touched by taint of action. [V:7]

The man who is united with the Divine, the knower of Truth, thinks, "I do nothing at all." For in seeing, hearing, touching, smelling, eating, moving, sleeping, breathing. [V:8]

In speaking, giving, seizing, opening and closing the eyes, he holds that only the senses move among the objects of the senses. [V:9]

The man who is united with the Divine, abandoneth attachment to the fruits of action and attaineth to eternal peace. But he whose soul is not in union with the divine, is impelled by desire and is attached to the fruit of action and is (therefore) bound. [V:12]

Sages look with an equal eye on a Brahmin, adorned with learning and humility, or a cow, or an elephant, and even on a dog and a *pariah* (outcaste). [V:18]

He who, even here, before he leaves his body, is able to resist the rush of desire and anger, he is with God united. He is the happy man. [V:23]

Whose happiness is within, whose joy is within, whose light is within, that *yogi*, becoming divine, attains the beatitude of God (*Brahmanirvana*). [V:24]

He who does the work which it is his duty to do but seeks no gain from work, no reward, that man is a *sanyasi* and a *yogi*: not he who lights no sacrificial fire and performs no ceremonies. [VI:1]

Let a man lift his self by the Self (*Atman*): let him not degrade himself. For, verily, is the Self the only friend of the self, and the Self alone is the enemy of the self. [VI:5]

The *yogi*, whose soul is satisfied with wisdom and knowledge (*gnana* and *vignana*), unwavering, whose senses are subdued, to whom a clod, a stone and gold are the same, is said to be *yukta* (harmonised, controlled in *yoga*). [VI:8]

He who is equal-minded among friends, companions and foes, among strangers and neutrals, among aliens and kingsmen, among saints and sinners, he hath attained excellence. [VI:9]

In a pure place let him set his firm seat, not too much raised, nor yet too low, covered with *kusha* grass, a deer skin and a cloth, one over the other. [VI:11]

There, steady on his seat, making his mind one-pointed and restraining his thought and sense, let him practise *yoga* for the purification of the soul. [VI:12]

Holding the body, head and neck, erect and still, gazing fixedly at the tip of his nose, without looking around. [VI:13]

Serene and fearless, firm in the vow of *brahmacharya*, the mind controlled, let him sit, harmonised, his mind turned to Me and aspiring after Me alone. [VI:14]

Verily, *yoga* is not for him who eateth too much, nor for him who abstains too much from eating. Nor is *yoga* for him who sleepeth too much, nor for him who keeps awake too much, O Arjuna! [VI:16]

As often as the wavering and unsteady mind runneth away, so often let the man restrain and bring it back to the control of the Self alone. [VI:26]

His self harmonised by *yoga*, he seeth the One Self abiding in all beings in the One Self: everywhere he seeth the same (One Ancient Self). [VI:29]

He who seeth Me everywhere and seeth everything in Me, to him I am not lost and he is not lost to Me.

[VI:30]

For the mind is, verily, fickle, O Krishna! It is turbulent, strong and obstinate. I deem it as hard to control as the wind. [VI:34]

Without doubt, O Arjuna, the mind is hard to curb and the mind is restless. But it can be curbed by constant practice (*abhayasa*) and by dispassion (*vairagya*). [VI:35]

He, who is unsubdued, though he has faith (*Shraddha*), he whose mind wanders away from *yoga* and fails to attain perfection in *yoga*, what way does he go, O Krishna? [VI:37]

O Arjuna, neither in this life nor in the life to come is there destruction for such a man; for never doth any who worketh righteousness, O beloved, tread the path of woe. [VI:40]

Having attained to the worlds of the righteous and having dwelt there, for very many years, the *yoga-bhrishta* is born again in a pure and prosperous house. [VI:41]

There he recovers the insight (the mental impressions of union with the Divine) acquired in his former life, Arjuna, and so he strives anew for the attainment of perfection. [VI:43]

Verily, the *yogi*, labouring with assiduity, purified from sin, perfecting himself through many lives, reacheth the supreme goal. [VI:45]

The *yogi* is greater than the ascetic; the *yogi* is greater even than the Vedic scholar; the *yogi* is greater than the man of ritual works. Therefore, do thou become a *yogi*, O Arjuna! [VI:46]

Among thousands of men, scarce one striveth for perfection: and among those who strive and win, scarce one doth know Me as I am in truth. [VII:3]

There is naught whatsoever higher than I, O Arjuna!

All that is here is threaded on Me as rows of pearls are threaded on a single string. [VII:7]

I am the fresh taste in the waters, O Arjuna, and the light in the moon and the sun. I am the One Word of worship (Om) in all the Vedas. I am the sound in ether and the seed of strength in men. [VII:8]

Of four kinds are the virtuous ones who worship Me: the man who suffers, the man who yearns for knowledge, the man who seeks wealth, and the man of wisdom, O Arjuna! [VII:16]

All these are noble, but I deem the wise as verily Myself. For, being completely harmonised, he regards Me as the Goal Supreme. [VII:18]

At the end of many births, the man grown wise cometh to Me, knowing that the Lord (Vasudeva) is all that is. Such a *mahatma* (great soul) is rarely found. [VII:19]

But transient is the fruit that comes to those small-minded men. These, the worshippers of the gods, go to the gods. But they who worship Me, My devotees, come unto Me. [VII:23]

He who casting off the body, goeth forth, meditating upon Me alone, at the hour of death, he attaineth to My State (*madbhavam*). Doubt that not! [VIII:5]

Whosoever, O Arjuna, abandoneth the body, thinking upon any being (*bhavam*), to that being (or object) only he goeth, ever absorbed in its thought. [VIII:6]

Therefore, at all times, think of Me and fight! When thy mind and understanding are set on Me, thou shalt surely come to Me. [VIII:7]

Arjuna, he who constantly thinketh upon Me with a mind that regardeth none else, he, the *yogi nitya-yuktah* (ever harmonised, always absorbed in Me), he easily attaineth Me. [VIII:14]

Such perfect men, great souls, *mahatmas*, having come to Me, come not again to birth, the place of pain, impermanent: they have gone to the highest Bliss (the highest Perfection). [VIII:15]

Arjuna, all the worlds, upto the *Brahmaloka*, they appear and disappear; they come and go. But he who cometh unto Me, he knoweth birth no more. [VIII:16]

Having enjoyed the vast world of heaven, when their merit is exhausted, they come back to this world of death. Thus following the words of the three Vedas and desirous of enjoyments, they obtain the passing (what is subject to birth and death). [IX:21]

But, those who worship Me and meditate on Me alone, to them who are self-controlled, I give what they have not and hold secure whatever they have. [IX:22]

He who offereth to Me with devotion a leaf, a flower, a fruit, or water, that gift of love I accept (as offering) of the pure of heart. [IX:26]

Whatever thou doest, whatever thou eatest, whatever thou offerest, whatever thou givest away, whatever austerities thou dost practise, let it all be done, O Arjuna, as an offering unto Me. [IX:27]

So shalt thou be freed from the bonds of action, from good and evil fruits (of deeds). With thy mind firmly set on the way of renunciation, thou shalt be free and come to Me. [IX:28]

Even if a man, deep-sunk in sin, worships Me with single heart, he, too, must be reckoned as righteous, for he hath rightly resolved. [IX:30]

Fix thy mind on Me; be devoted to Me; worship Me; bow down to Me. Thus having controlled thyself, and making Me thy goal supreme, thou shalt come unto Me. [IX:34]

Arjuna said:

How may I know Thee, O Yogin, by constant meditation? In what aspects art Thou, O Blessed Lord, to be thought of by me? [X:17]

Recount to me again and at length of Thy yogic power and glory; for I am never satiated with drinking the nectar of Thy speech. [X:18]

The Blessed Lord said:

So be it, Arjuna! I will declare to thee (some) of My forms divine, only those which are prominent; for there is no end to My extent. [X:19]

I am the Self, O Arjuna, seated in the hearts of all creatures. I am the beginning, the middle, and also the end of all beings. [X:20]

And know, O Arjuna, that I am the Seed of all beings. Nor is there anything, moving or unmoving, that can exist with Me. [X:39]

There is no end to My divine manifestations, O Arjuna. What has been spoken by Me is only illustrative of My infinite glory. [X:40]

Whatsoever being there is, endowed with glory and beauty and strength, know that to have sprung from a fraction of My splendour. [X:41]

But of what use to thee, O Arjuna, is this detailed knowledge? I sustain this whole universe, pervading it with but one fragment of Myself: and I abide! [X:42]

Arjuna said:

Thou art, O Lord Supreme, as Thou dost say Thou art. Yet I desire to see Thy divine form, O *Purushottama* (Person Supreme)! [XI:3]

The Blessed Lord said:

Behold, O Arjuna, My forms by hundreds and by thousands, various in kind, divine, of innumerable colours and shapes. [XI:5]

Behold here today, O Arjuna, the whole universe with all things that move and move not, and whatever else

thou desirest to see, all concentrated in My Body.
[XI:7]

But, verily, thou canst not behold Me with these thine (mortal) eyes; (so) I give unto thee the divine eye. Behold My sovereign *Yoga* (divine power and glory).
[XI:8]

With myriad mouths and eyes, with myriad visions of marvel, with myriad divine ornaments and countless godly weapons all upraised;
[XI:10]

Wearing celestial garlands and vestures, anointed with heavenly perfumes, full of all marvels, resplendent, boundless, with face turned everywhere.
[XI:11]

Could but a thousand suns blaze forth all at once in the sky, it would be like the splendour of that exalted Being.
[XI:12]

There did Arjuna behold the whole universe, with its manifold divisions blended into one, in the body of the God of gods.
[XI:13]

Then, he, Arjuna, sore amazed, his hair standing on end, bowed down his head to the Lord and with folded hands said:
[XI:14]

Yea! Now I see how all is wrapt in Thee!
The gods are in Thy glorious frame, O Lord!
Brahma upon his lotus-throne, and all
The sages and the Serpent Powers divine!
[XI:15]

Thou Lord of all! I see Thy arms and breasts,
Thy faces and Thine eyes on every side,
In Form diversified, yet I see not
Thy centre nor beginning nor Thy end!   [XI:16]

Thou art the *aksharam* — the One Supreme:
Thou art the resting-place of all this world:
Thou art the Undying Guardian of the Law:
Thou art, I hold, the Immemorial Man!   [XI:18]

This space from bound to bound, from pole to pole,
Is full of Thee alone: all space is full!
At sight of this, Thy awful, wonder-form.
The triple worlds sink down, O Mighty One!   [XI:20]

Thy mighty Form of many mouths and eyes,
Of things and feet innumerate, and arms
So vast, and countless bosoms, countless teeth,
The worlds behold and tremble, so do I!   [XI:23]

Into thy gaping mouths, tremendous toothed
And terrible to see, they hurrying rush —   [XI:26]

All sons of Dhritarashtra and, with them,
The hosts of kings and Bhishma, Karna, Dron,
And all the noblest warriors of our hosts,
Some caught between the teeth are seen with heads
All mangled, crushed and ground to dust and death
Between Thy jaws they lie — the best of both! [XI:27]

As moths which swiftly flutter to a light —
A blazing fire — to meet their doom, so do
These men, with headlong speed, rush in to meet
Their doom of death within Thy flaming mouths!

[XI:29]

Ah Vishnu! tell me who Thou art: why is
Thy Form so full of awe? I worship Thee:
Have mercy, God Supreme! I wish to know
Thee, Primal One! For I know not Thy ways!   [XI:31]

Lo, Time am I, world-wrecker Time am I!
The Slayer Time, now ready for the hour
That ripens to the ruin of all these hosts:
E'en if thou flee, all these shall cease to be!   [XI:32]

Arise thou, then! Obtain renown! Fight thou
Thy foes! The kingdom awaits thee. By Me –
Not thee — they all are slain: seem thou to slay!
Be thou My instrument! But strike, O knight!   [XI:33]

Strike thou at Drona! And at Bhishma strike!
At Karna, too, and Jayadratha — all
The warriors here: know I do bid them die!
Be not afraid! Fight thou and slay the slain!   [XI:34]

Arjuna said:

Thou art the first of gods: th' Eternal Man
Thou art: in Thee the cosmos safe abides!
The knower and the known — the twain in One
Art Thou! Our Goal Supreme: in Thee is all!   [XI:38]

All hail to Thee in front, behind! And hail
On every side! O All! In pow'r and strength,
O Boundless One! Alone, Thou roundest all:
Thou One in all and, therefore, Thou art All!   [XI:40]

Sometimes, in rashness, did I speak to Thee:
I thought of Thee my "friend" and, unaware   [XI:41]

Of this Thy greatness, called Thee "Krishna!" "Prince!"
Or "Comrade!" Out of fondness or at play,
Or on the bed or seated or at meals,
Alone or in the throng, I did Thee wrong,
O Sinless One! For this I pray to Thee,
   "Forgive! Forgive my faults! Eternal Lord!"   [XI:42]

For now I know Thou art the Father great
Of all below, of all above, of all
The worlds within! The Guru, Teacher Thou,
Adorable as no one else in all
The worlds: there is none equal unto Thee!
How then could any one in all the worlds
Be greater than Thy glory past compare?
Thou art the Highest, Lord, I worship Thee!   [XI:43]

With body bent and reverent, I bow
And seek Thy grace, O Lord adorable!
As father with the son, as friend with friend,
As lover with beloved, bear with me!   [XI:44]

I have seen That which none hath seen before —
The marvel of Thy form! My heart is glad,

Yet filled with fear! O Lord of Gods! Retake
Thine earthly shape which earthly eyes may bear!

[XI:45]

The Blessed Lord said:

Yet not by the Vedas, nor by austerities, nor by gifts,
nor by sacrifices, can I be seen in the Form in which
thou hast seen Me.   [XI:53]

But by devotion to Me alone, devotion undivided — may
I thus be known and seen in essence, and entered into,
O Arjuna!   [XI:54]

Who doeth work for Me, who maketh Me his supreme
goal, he, My devotee, freed from attachment, without
ill-will towards any creature, he cometh unto Me, O
Arjuna!   [XI:55]

Arjuna said:

Those devotees who, ever harmonised, worship Thee,
and those again who worship the Indestructible, the
Unmanifested, of these, who is the more learned in
yoga?   [XII:1]

The Blessed Lord said:

They who, fixing their minds on Me, worship Me, ever
harmonised and endowed with faith supreme, them do
I hold as the best *yogis*.   [XII:2]

They who worship the Indestructible, the Indefinable,

the Unmanifested, the Omnipresent, the Unthinkable, the Unchanging, the Immutable, the Constant. [XII:3]

(They who worship thus), restraining their senses, regarding everything equally, rejoicing in the welfare of all beings, they also come unto Me. [XII:4]

On Me alone fix thy mind and let thy understanding dwell in Me. And without doubt thou shalt live hereafter in Me alone. [XII:8]

But if thou art not able firmly to fix thy mind on Me, then seek to reach Me, O Arjuna, by the *yoga* of constant practice (of concentration). [XII:9]

If thou art unable even to practice (concentration), then be intent on My service. Perform actions for My sake, and thou shalt attain perfection. [XII:10]

If even to do this thou hast not the strength, then renounce all fruit of action, seeking refuge in devotion to Me, holding thyself in control. [XII:11]

Better, indeed, is knowledge than constant practice (of concentration); meditation is better than knowledge; better than meditation is renunciation of the fruit of action; on renunciation follows peace. [XII:12]

He who beareth no ill-will to any being, is friendly and compassionate, free from egoism and self-sense, in pain and pleasure has poised mind, is forgiving;
[XII:13]

The *yogi* who is ever content, ever in harmony and master of himself, resolute, with mind and understanding dedicated to Me, he, My devotee, is My beloved.

[XII:14]

He by whom the world is not disturbed and who is not disturbed by the world, who is freed from the agitations of joy and anger and fear, he is My beloved.

[XII:15]

He who is ambition-less, is pure, skilful in action, is passionless and free from fear, he who renounces the fruit of every undertaking to Me, he My *bhakta* (devotee), is My beloved.   [XII:16]

He who neither rejoiceth nor hateth nor grieveth nor craveth, he who renounceth good and ill, he, My devout worshipper, is My beloved.   [XII:17]

Alike to foe and friend, alike in fame and ignominy, alike in cold and heat, in pleasure and pain, freed from attachment,   [XII:18]

Taking equally praise and blame, silent, content with what cometh, homeless, of steady mind, he, My devout worshipper, is My beloved.   [XII:19]

They, verily, who worship this *dharma* (law) of immortality, as taught herein, and, endowed with faith, believe in Me as the Supreme, they, My *bhaktas*, are My beloved.   [XII:20]

He who sees the Supreme Lord dwelling alike in all beings, the Imperishable within the perishable, he truly sees. [XIII:27]

He who sees that all actions are performed by *Prakriti* (nature) and that the Self is actionless, he truly sees. [XIII:29]

When he perceives that the diverse forms of life are all rooted in the One and are spread forth from the One, then he attains Brahman. [XIII:30]

The Imperishable Supreme Self, O Arjuna, is without beginning and without qualities. And though He is seated in the body, yet He acteth not nor is He affected by action. [XIII:31]

As ether, though present everywhere, is not tainted, by reason of its subtlety, so the Self, though seated everywhere in the body, is free from taint. [XIII:32]

He to whom pleasure and pain are alike, who is centred in his Self, to whom clod or stone or gold are one, who is same to loved and unloved, whose mind is steady, who remains the same in censure and in praise; [XIV:24]

He who looks equally upon honour and dishonour and is the same to friend and foe, who has abandoned all ambition, he is said to have crossed over the *gunas*. [XIV:25]

He, who serveth Me with unswerving devotion, passes beyond the *gunas* and becomes one with Brahman.

[XIV:26]

They go to that Indestructible Home, who have no pride and no delusion (*moha*), who victorious rise over the vice of attachment, who dwell constantly in the *Adhyatman* (the Self within), whose desires have departed, who have been liberated from the *dvandas* (pairs of opposites) of pleasure and pain.

[XV:5]

Nor sun, nor moon, nor fire shineth there: nor any one who goeth there ever returneth. It is My supreme Abode.

[XV:6]

Triple is gateway of this hell, destructive of the self, lust, wrath and greed. Therefore let men shun these three.

[XVI:21]

The foods which prolong life and promote purity, strength, health, joy and cheerfulness, which are sweet, soft, nourishing and agreeable, are liked by *sattvic* men.

[XVII:8]

The foods that are bitter, sour, salted, over-hot, pungent, dry and burning, and which produce pain, grief and disease are liked by the *rajasic* men.

[XVII:9]

That which is stale, tasteless, putrid, rotten, unclean, is the food liked by the *tamasic* men.

[XVII:10]

Speech that hurts no one, that is truthful, pleasant and beneficial, and the constant study of the sacred books, this is said to be the *tapas* (austerity) of speech. [XVII:15]

Serenity of mind, gentleness, silence, self-restraint, purity of thought (and feeling), this is called the *tapas* (austerity) of mind. [XVII:16]

The gift which is given, from a sense of duty, to one from whom nothing in return is expected, and which is given in the right place at the right time to a deserving person, such a gift is *sattvic* (pure). [XVII:20]

When a gift is given with a view to receiving something in return or with expectation of a future reward, or when it is given unwillingly, such a gift is *rajasic* (passionate). [XVII:21]

The gift which is given at a wrong place or time or to an unworthy person, or with disrespect or contempt, such a gift is *tamasic* (dark). [XVII:22]

"*Om Tat Sat,*" this is considered to be the threefold designation of Brahman. By this were ordained of old the Brahmins, the Vedas and the sacrifices. [XVII:23]

Therefore all acts of sacrifice, gift and austerity, enjoined in the scriptures, are always begun with the utterance of "*Om*" by the men who know Brahman. [XVII:24]

Those who seek liberation, begin their acts of sacrifice, austerity and gift with the utterance of "*Tat*" ("That"), without thought of reward. [XVII:25]

The word "*Sat*" is used in the sense of reality and goodness. Likewise, O Arjuna, the word "*Sat*" is used for praiseworthy action. [XVII:26]

Steadfastness in sacrifice, austerity and gift is also, called "*Sat*"; and so also action consecrated to That is called "*Sat*". [XVII:27]

Whatsoever is done without faith, whether it be offering (in sacrifice), gift or austerity, or anything else, is called *asat*. O Arjuna! Such work is of no value hereafter or here. [XVII:28]

Arjuna said:

I desire, O Krishna, to know the truth about *sanyasa* (renunciation) and about *tyaga* (relinquishment).
[XVIII:1]

The Blessed Lord said:

The sages understand by renunciation (*sanyasa*) giving up of desire-prompted works; the giving up of the fruits of all actions is called relinquishment (*tyaga*) by the wise.
[XVIII:2]

Deeds of sacrifice, almsgiving and austerity should not be given up, but should be performed. For sacrifice, almsgiving and austerity are purifiers of the wise.
[XVIII:5]

But even these actions should be done, leaving aside attachment and fruit. This, O Arjuna, is my decided and final view. [XVIII:6]

Learn of Me, O Arjuna, these five causes, for the accomplishment of all action, as declared in the *Sankhya* doctrine. [XVIII:13]

The seat of action (the body), the agent, the various organs, the diverse kinds of efforts, and providence, being the fifth. [XVIII:14]

That being so, the man of perverse mind who, on account of his untrained understanding, looks upon himself as the sole agent (or actor), verily he seeth not! [XVIII:16]

He who is free from the egoistic notion, whose *buddhi* (understanding) is not sullied, though he slay these people, he slayeth not, nor is bound (by his actions). [XVIII:17]

Man reacheth perfection, by each being devoted to his own duty. Listen thou, how perfection is won by him who is devoted to his own duty. [XVIII:45]

He from Whom is the arising (emanation) of all beings and by Whom all this (creation) is pervaded, by worshipping Him through doing his own duty, doth man attain perfection. [XVIII:46]

Surrendering in thought all action to Me, regarding Me as the Supreme, taking refuge in *buddhi-yoga*, the *yoga* of discrimination, do thou fix thy thought ever on Me.
[XVIII:57]

Thinking on Me, thou shalt cross over all obstacles by My Grace. But if, from egoism, thou wilt not listen (to Me), thou shalt perish.
[XVIII:58]

If, entrenched in egoism, thou thinkest, "I will not fight," know that thy resolve is vain. Nature will constrain thee!
[XVIII:59]

O Arjuna, bound by thine own acts, born of thine own nature, that which, through delusion, thou wishest not to do, even that helplessly thou shalt perform.
[XVIII:60]

The Lord dwelleth in the hearts of all beings, O Arjuna, causing them to revolve by *maya* (His power), as if they were mounted on a machine.
[XVIII:61]

Flee unto Him for shelter with all being, O Arjuna! By His grace thou shalt obtain Supreme Peace, the Eternal Abode.
[XVIII:62]

Fix thy mind on Me; be devoted to Me; sacrifice to Me; prostrate thyself before Me. So shalt thou come to Me. I pledge thee My troth; thou art dear to Me!
[XVIII:65]

Abandoning all duties, come unto Me alone for shelter. Grieve not! I shall liberate thee from all sins.

[XVIII:66]

He who declares this supreme secret to My devotees, showing the highest devotion for Me, he, without doubt, shall come to Me.

[XVIII:68]

Nor is there any among men who does dearer service to Me that he. Nor shall there be another dearer to Me on earth than he.

[XVIII:69]

Sanjaya said:

Wherever is Krishna, the Lord of Yoga, wherever is Arjuna, the archer, assured are there prosperity, victory, welfare and *neeti* (righteousness or morality).

[XVIII: 78]

Sri Krishnarpanam astu
Shubham Bhavantu

To the Blessed Krishna be homage!
May there be happiness everywhere!

Note: The English translation of the *slokas* is from:

The Bhagavad Gita: The Song of Life
By Sadhu Vaswani

Published By:
Gita Publishing House
Sadhu Vaswani Mission
10, Sadhu Vaswani Path,
Pune – 411 001 (India).
gph@sadhuvaswani.org
www.dadavaswanisbooks.org

Other Books on The Bhagavad Gita....

The Heart of The Gita

By Sadhu Vaswani
Price: ₹ 60

7 Commandments of the Bhagavad Gita

By J.P. Vaswani
Price: ₹ 250

The Bhagavad Gita: The Song of the Supreme

By Sadhu Vaswani
Price: ₹ 70

The Bhagavad Gita: The Song of Life

By Sadhu Vaswani
Price: ₹ 100